THE BATTERSEA SHIELD

The Battersea Shield

I.M.STEAD

Published for the Trustees of the British Museum
by British Museum Publications Limited

Published by British Museum Publications Limited
46 Bloomsbury Street, London WC1B 3QQ

British Library Cataloguing in Publication Data
Stead, I.M.
    The Battersea Shield.
    1. Battersea Shield
    I. Title
    739.7′52′09362   NK6643

ISBN 0-7141-1375-1

Set in 10 on 11pt Ehrhardt by Bookworm Typesetting, Salford.

Jacket designed by Norman Ball

Printed in Great Britain by Paradigm Print,
Gateshead, Tyne and Wear
Plates Printed by the University Press, Oxford

Contents

List of Illustrations

Preface

At first sight it is surprising that the much-praised Battersea shield – 'the noblest creation of Late Celtic art' (Holmes 1907: 244) – has never been the subject of a detailed publication. But in order to study an object of this complexity it is essential to work in the institution which houses it. Only then can one devote the necessary amount of time to the object, take it apart and reassemble it, and have close liaison with illustrator, photographer, conservation officer and scientist. The way for this study was paved by the Trustees' decision to expand the Department of Prehistoric and Romano-British Antiquities by appointing not only an Assistant Keeper (1974) but also a Research Assistant (1975) to curate the Iron Age antiquities. Previous staff had had far wider responsibilities. But even a full-time specialist on the Iron Age would normally be daunted by the prospect of writing a monograph on the Battersea shield. That problem had to be faced when the Trustees decided to allow it to travel to Austria for an exhibition 'The Celts in Central Europe', at Hallein from 1 May to 30 September 1980. It was the first occasion on which the shield had left the British Museum since its purchase 123 years previously, and the Trustees rightly insisted that it should be thoroughly examined and recorded, and the report prepared for publication. The examination and detailed record was completed in April 1980: with the assistance of Peter Shorer the components were removed from their mount, and then drawn by Robert Pengelly, photographed by Peter Hayman and examined again in the Research Laboratory by Paul Craddock.

C.F.C. Hawkes, E.M. Jope, J.V.S. Megaw and M.G. Spratling read drafts of parts of the text, which has benefited considerably from their criticisms; they do not agree with all the views expressed here and Hawkes, in particular, in a long correspondence has patiently insisted on a late date (c. 25–15 BC). The Battersea shield is unique, and assessment of its date is subjective, but this paper attempts to present all the evidence to enable the reader to form his own judgement.

Discovery

In 1857 the British Museum purchased from Henry Briggs and ... Austin, for the sum of £40, the bronze facing of a shield (57.7-15.1) and a 'bronze ornament, probably the covering of the handle of the shield' (57.7-15.2) found in the Thames near Battersea. Briggs, described in one entry as a labourer, made a steady income selling artefacts mainly or exclusively from the Thames – on forty-three occasions between 1843 and 1866 he sold single items or small collections to the British Museum.

The shield was first mentioned in print in a short paper describing objects from the Thames which were exhibited on 10 March 1858 to the British Archaeological Association by their honorary secretary, H. Syer Cuming (1858). That paper included a note by Thomas Bateman about some of his own recent acquisitions from the river, in which he mentions the base of a cauldron which he did not purchase because the owner thought it was a shield and so attached an undue value to it. Cuming accepted that object as a cauldron, but added that 'the locality has produced a veritable Celtic shield ... now deposited in the British Museum'. The account is tantalising, and it is obvious that the shield was not exhibited with the other finds, being included here almost as an afterthought. Its provenance is recorded as from the same locality as 'a few specimens dredged up from the bed of the river, near to the new bridge' (Chelsea Suspension Bridge).

An earlier note by Cuming (1857: 237-8) shows how difficult it was to establish the exact provenance of a river find. He refers to the discovery of human remains and weapons – but 'the facts which have come to my knowledge are so few and fragmentary that they serve rather to incite than to satisfy inquiry. So far as I have been able to collect, there has been found in the Thames during a period of several months, certainly extending from December 1854 until October 1855, numerous human crania, of *two distinct types*, mingled with weapons of *bronze* and *iron*. The exact spot where these remains were discovered has been most jealously concealed by both workmen and curiosity dealers, but by dint of vigilant inquiry, and the employment of means which it is not necessary to detail, I have so far succeeded in unravelling the mystery, as to leave no doubt upon my mind that the locality in question is *Battersea*, and that the *reliquiae* were brought to light whilst constructing the foundations of the piers for the support of the new suspension bridge across the Thames'. Apparently 'the skulls and weapons were scattered from the Middlesex shore to about the middle of the river, where the greater quantity were found'.

Description

The remains consist of several pieces of bronze which formed the facing of a shield made of organic materials (Fig. 1). There are three *panels* ornamented in repoussé and with added *roundels*; the panels are attached by *rivets* some of which pass through the four background *sheets* which occupy the quadrants of the shield. The whole is surrounded by *binding-strips*, and a separate piece of bronze was used as the cover for the *handle*.

i *The Panels*

A The central circular panel (Fig. 2; Pl. I) is 286 – 290 mm in diameter with two small perforated tags appended at either side to give an overall width of 294 mm. It is composed of two pieces: the broad flange with repoussé ornament, and the central boss which is attached to the flange by eight rivets.

The central boss is 101 – 103 mm in diameter and rises to 42 mm above the level of the flange. Its rim is seated within a raised cordon on the flange, and the extremely neat junction appears as a concentric groove on the upper surface. It has been so well polished that the rivet-heads are hardly distinguishable on top. On the underside the junction is neat but obvious, and no attempt has been made to disguise the rivets (Pl. IIIb). The boss is hemispherical with a grooved and cordoned dished setting for a large decorative roundel. Marks of a planishing hammer are clearly visible on the underside.

The decoration on the broad flange, and on Panels B and C, is executed in very fine high and complex repoussé-work. The designs rise from the flat at steep angles and often culminate in sharp ridges. The basic forms are elaborated by subsidiary shapes, dished and raised, in a way which defies reproduction in a line-drawing. Additional variety is provided by minor details such as punched infilling and tooled surfaces left deliberately unpolished: such features have been omitted from the line-drawings but can be appreciated in the photographs.

The design is symmetrical, and it will be described by imagining a vertical line through the centre and then viewing one half from the side – with the boss at the top and the small perforated tag at the bottom (Fig. 3; Pl. IIa). The motif which is then central is derived from a palmette, incorporating a roundel on each side of the stem. The lobe which surmounts the central stem, and the triangular shape above it, have been left unpolished with very fine planishing marks clearly visible, but the areas to either side of the lobe have been decorated with punched dots. These details are much more obvious in the right half of the panel, where the lobe is a long way from being central to

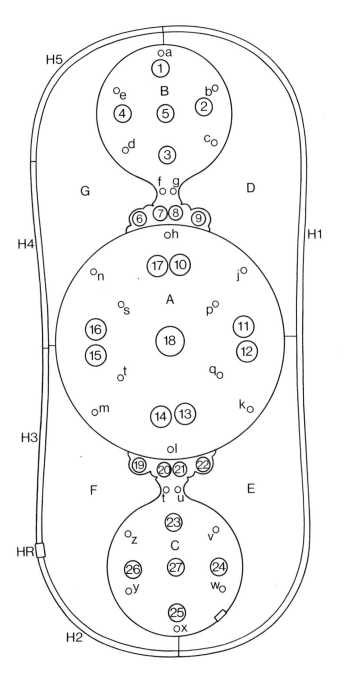

Figure 1. Battersea shield: showing the letters and numbers used in the description.

Figure 2. Battersea shield: Panel A (for section A-A1 see Fig.16a).

11

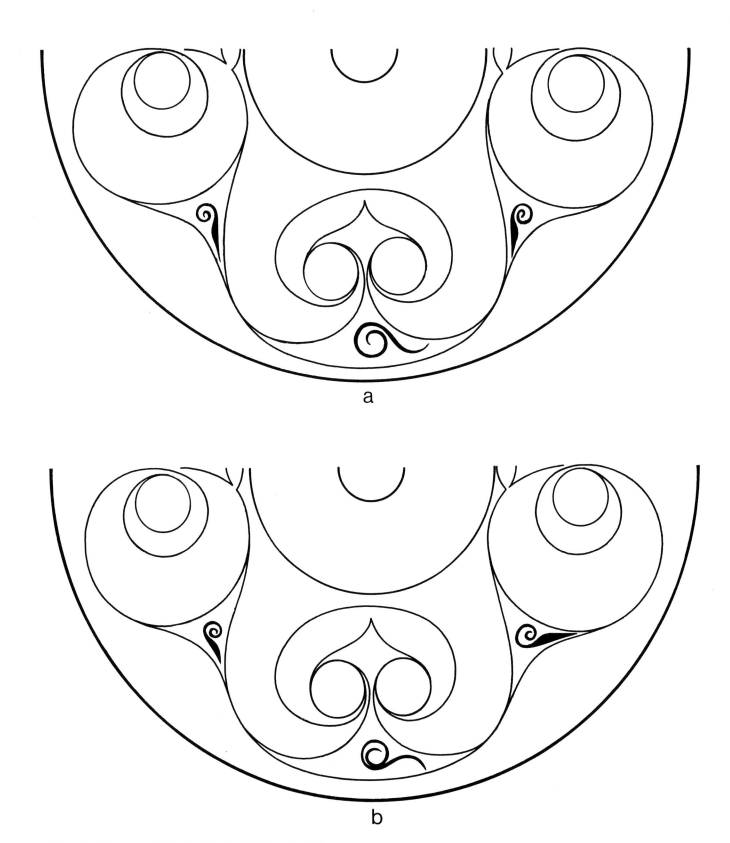

a

b

Figure 3. Battersea shield: Panel A, details. Showing differences
in detail in each half: a. right half; b. left half.

the triangle (Pl. IIIa); in the left half of the panel these areas are pitted with corrosion. Below the stem is a 'triangular' area with concave sides above and convex below, enclosing raised motifs which differ slightly (Fig. 3). In the right half of the panel this motif is larger, and better fills the space: it springs from a curved stem from the right corner of the triangle which spirals round to terminate in a comma-like form with a ridged crown, whilst an interlocking comma rises from within the spiral. The top and left angles of the triangle are filled with simple arcs. In the left half of the panel the motif is smaller, and the stem is again in the right corner – although exact fold-over symmetry requires it in the left corner; it curves upwards, instead of downwards, and the infilling arcs on the opposite side run together instead of facing one another (Pl. IVa). The ridged crown of the comma is bordered by a row of punched dots, and in the left half of the panel (but not in the right) there are similar punched dots on the stem which encircles the comma. In the left half, at the bottom right of the 'triangular' area, is a further row of similar punch-marks – an irregular line of closely spaced dots.

From each side of the 'triangular' base of the palmette a sharply ridged line curves upwards and divides to form one angle of a raised triangular shape surmounted by a 'snail-shell' spiral. The triangle has concave sides, and from its other two angles similar sharply ridged lines curve away to create a circular shape. The entire panel has four similar triangles, each with a snail-shell spiral, and in each the snail-shell clearly emanates from one corner of the triangle whilst the other two corners are occupied by arcs – similar to the design in the triangles below the palmettes. In the right half the arrangement is symmetrical: both snail-shells spring from the bottom angle and are set back to back, with one wound clockwise and the other anti-clockwise (Fig. 3a; Pl. IVb). In the left half the arrangement is quite different and not symmetrical. The snail-shell to the right of the palmette springs from the angle on the right, not from the bottom; but the one to the left of the palmette stems from the bottom and faces the palmette (Fig. 3b). Both snail-shells in the left half are wound clockwise. Where the surface is uncorroded rows of punched dots can be distinguished both on the stems and round the spirals of the snail-shells, and within the surrounding triangular field some of the surface has been left unpolished (perhaps because the areas were difficult to polish, but elsewhere unpolished areas were left for effect).

The rest of the design on the central panel is better described when viewed from the centre looking upwards or downwards – with the overall design divided horizontally instead of vertically (Pl. IIb). The large circular shapes stemming from the triangles surmounted by snail-shells are thus juxtaposed, and have the appearance of a bespectacled face with roundels providing a pair of close-set 'eyes' and repoussé ornament forming 'lips' below and 'eyebrows' above. The upper borders of the 'spectacle-frames' curve down and round to enclose the 'eyes' from above, whereas below the borders meet at a sharp point above the 'lips'. The triangular areas above the 'lips' have visible tool-marks and may have been left

unpolished for effect. Each 'eye' is an inset roundel: its rounded border swells markedly on the outside and is crowned by a ridge bordered outside by a row of punched dots – a feature which is particularly clear on the surrounds of roundel 14 (Pl. Va). Above the 'spectacles' an 'eyebrow' motif springs from an expanding stem rising from the junction of the 'eyes'. This curved shape, which spreads over the 'spectacles' resembles the shape ('forehead' and 'horns') over the 'animal-heads' on the immediately adjoining parts of Panels B and C.

Ten holes have been drilled through Panel A to take rivets to attach it to the organic part of the shield. Most are 2.6 mm in diameter: three (j, l and m) are slightly larger and oval, but there is no clear indication that they were re-drilled. In the corrosion around the rivet-holes on the upper surface are the impressions of the large domed rivet-heads from 6 to 7 mm in diameter, but they are not sharply defined. On the underside around rivet-hole k there is a very clear impression of a projecting 'tongue' from one of the underlying bronze sheets (Pl. Vb), but the tongue itself does not now survive (it would have been on Sheet E, see p. 18). Another feature on the underside is the slight circular impression from 10 to 14 mm across around several of the other rivet-holes (including polished areas round j, p, q and s), presumably caused by pressure from the domed head above rather than from the presence of a washer below. The drilled holes for the rivets to attach the roundels are much smaller, about 1.2 mm across.

Two roundels are missing from Panel A, and others have lost some 'enamel'. Otherwise damage is confined to a crack about 18 mm long, between one of the 'lip' motifs and the cordon surrounding the central boss.

B The circular panel with appendage from the upper part of the shield is 168 – 169 mm in diameter and 231 mm long. It is described following the orientation in Fig. 4 and Pls VI and VII, inverted from its position on the shield to facilitate exact comparison with Panel C.

The circular part of Panel B has a very narrow flange bordering a broad rounded cordon. At the top the cordon projects to form the base of the appended decoration, and its much broader flange with bordering groove is shaped to curve first concave and then convex, with a knick between the two. The appended decoration may be conveniently described as an 'animal-head', whose 'snout' – two super-imposed lobes – surmounts the main circular cordon. Above the 'snout' is a pelta whose terminals enclose inset roundels (7 and 8) – 'eyes' – and whose stem is crowned by an elongated pelta – 'forehead' – which terminates in spreading 'horns' or 'antlers', each enclosing another inset roundel (6 and the now empty 9). Each roundel has been riveted to the panel, and the missing one has a broken rivet and a second rivet-hole adjoining: at some time, presumably in antiquity, the roundel was replaced in a slightly different position. The repair seems to have been no more secure than the original attachment, and the roundel was subsequently lost.

The flange bordering the appendage continues round the 'horns' where it is very narrow indeed, and then curves outwards (followed by its groove) to form the ends of the

Figure 4. Battersea shield: Panel B.

0   5   10   15 CM

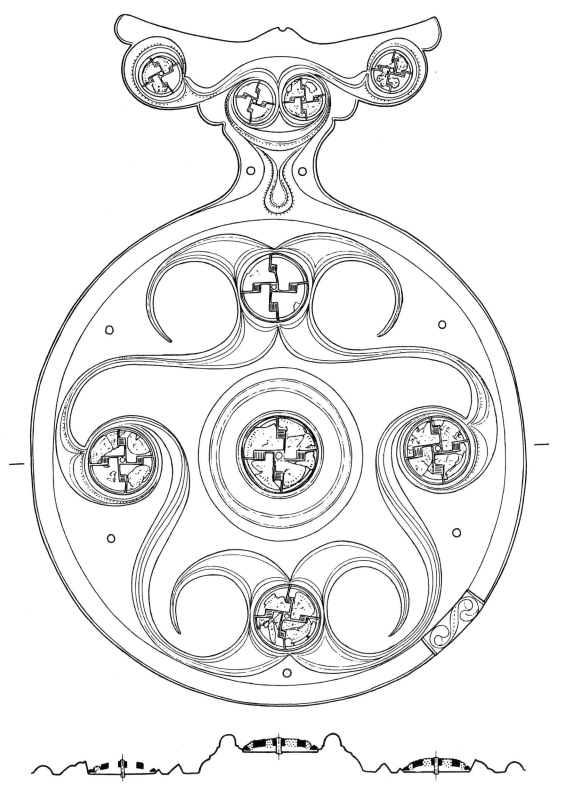

Figure 5. Battersea shield: Panel C. Scale as Fig. 4.

narrow overlap covered by the central Panel A. On the underside of these terminals and indeed elsewhere where the edges of the bronze sheets have been covered, the surface is well polished. Very fine tooling survives on the pelta-shapes and apparently also on the 'snout'. The sharp ridge round the top of the spreading 'horns' is bordered by a row of slight circular punch-marks, and so is the similar ridge under the lower pelta. The roundels forming the 'eyes' (7 and 8) are each tilted slightly away from the centre (Pl. VIIIa = Panel C); all other roundels are flat.

The design on the circular part of Panel B may be described as an arrangement of S-motifs around a central circle. There are four S-motifs, adjoining at top and bottom and interlocking at the sides. In the interlocking parts, and over the junctions, are inset roundels whose centres are arranged as the corners of a square set diagonally to the orientation of the shield. The pelta-like terminals of the S-motifs on the outer sides of roundels 2 and 4 may well have had tool-marks like those on Panel C (Pl. VIIIb), but the surfaces are obscured by slight corrosion-pitting. The inner edge of these peltas is bordered by a punched dotted line – clearly visible on the right and just distinguishable on the left. The terminals of the S-motifs at top and bottom are transformed by the overlying roundels into four trumpet forms with complex contours and an infilling of punched dots (Pl. IXa).

Panel B has been attached to the shield by seven rivets, and its upper edge for a length of 112 mm has been overlapped by up to 8 mm by the main circular Panel A. The rivet-holes are similar to those on Panel A. Three of them have been drilled twice, so that the hole is oval rather than circular: b and d may well have been re-drilled in antiquity, but the second drilling of c may be recent work. On the underside there are two 'tongue' impressions, highly polished by contact with the underlying sheets: that on the reverse at c is particularly clear, but a similar mark under d is less clear and has been clipped by the rivet-hole.

Apart from the lost roundel, and some red 'enamel' missing from other roundels, damage to Panel B includes: a hole up to 14 mm long and 2 mm wide on the stem of an S-motif to the bottom right of roundel 1; a crack by the stem of the S to the left of roundel 1; a crack round the border of the central circle to the top right of roundel 5; and cracks above and below roundels 1 and 3.

C This panel, very similar to but not exactly the same as Panel B, has a diameter of 169 – 171 mm and a total length of 224 mm (Fig. 5). The main differences between the two panels are:
(i) B has a much longer 'snout' to the appended 'animal-head' (2.45 mm as opposed to 2.05 mm) with the overall height of 'animal-head' being 59 mm compared with 52.5 mm, and the total exposed length of the panel 222.5 mm compared with 215 mm.
(ii) That part of the upper border covered by Panel A has a low central arch in Panel B compared with a much higher arch – whose edge is pierced by a rivet-hole – on Panel C.
(iii) The S-motifs on the circular part of Panel B are markedly off-centre to the alignment of the 'snout' of the 'animal'; on Panel C they are only very slightly offset, but

in the same direction.
(iv) The stems of the top two S-motifs are more curved in Panel B than the corresponding motifs on Panel C.
(v) There is the mark of only one projecting tongue on the underside of Panel C, under rivet-hole w.
(vi) Panel C has a repair on the rim: a 10 mm-long crack in the bordering cordon has been covered on the upper surface by a rectangular strip 25 mm long for which a setting has been neatly filed (Pl. IXb). The strip is attached by two rivets, whose heads have been carefully polished and disguised. On the underside an additional rivet-hole has not been used. The decoration on the repair is a repoussé S-motif with thick stem and rounded terminals which are wrapped round the two rivets. There are circular punch impressions down the centre of the stem and tiny hammer marks on the background – both features which can be matched in the decoration of the three panels. It is quite possible that the repair was carried out during the original manufacture.

Damage to Panel C includes an interrupted crack round the lower half of the circumference of the central circle, and cracks above and below roundels 23 and 25.

ii *The Roundels*

The shield is decorated with a series of bronze roundels with red 'enamel' inlay. Each of the three panels had nine roundels, of which twenty-four survive. Four different sizes were employed: those around Panel A, and on the circular parts of Panels B and C (including the centre of B but not the centre of C) are 23 – 24 mm in diameter; those on the appended 'animal-heads' of Panels B and C are 15 mm in diameter; and two larger roundels are at the centres of Panels C (26 mm) and A (31 mm). Each roundel has a circular bronze framework crossed by a swastika-like motif which defines four quadrants (Fig. 6a; Pl. Xa). The red 'enamel' is likely to have been attached in the following way (p. 49; Hughes 1972: 99): the bronze framework would have been inverted in a depression of the same size; soft, malleable 'enamel' would have been pressed into the hollow; the roundel would have been removed from the depression, riveted in position, and the 'enamel' polished on top.

The bronze frameworks were undoubtedly cast, by the *cire perdue* method, so that no two are exactly alike. Detailed study shows considerable variety, particularly in the square panels on the arms of the swastika – some are ornamented with dots but most are hatched with from two to five bars arranged clockwise or crosswise:

Type	Decoration in each square	Arrangement	Number of examples
A	5 bars	clockwise	1
B	5 bars	2 clockwise 2 crosswise	1
C*	4 bars	clockwise	5
D	4 bars	2 clockwise 2 crosswise	1
E	3 bars	clockwise	2
F	3 bars	crosswise	5
G	2 bars	crosswise	1
H	dot	–	2
* C1	4 bars in 3 squares, 5 bars in 1 square		5
C2	4 bars in 3 squares, 3 bars in 1 square		1
C3	4 bars in 2 squares, 5 bars in 2 squares		1

1 C	6 F	11 C1	16 C3	21 H	26 E
2 C1	7 F	12 C2	17 C	22 F	27 C
3 C	8 F	13 A†	18 B‡	23 D	
4 E	9 –	14 –	19 G	24 C	
5 C1	10 C1	15 C1	20 H	25 F	

† lacking the left square
‡ central square also has 5 bars

Table I To show the variation in the cast decoration on the frameworks of the roundels.

There has been a certain amount of movement of the roundels since the first photographs were taken, and one has been lost. The latter, the 'Missing Roundel', was recorded in position 17 on Reconstruction V, in position 11 on Reconstruction W, and its absence was noted first in 1969 at the time of Reconstruction X. Another roundel has been removed on several occasions: both front and back views were illustrated, off the shield, by Henry (1933: fig. 7, nos 2 and 4), and it is here called the 'Henry Roundel'. It was in position 11 on one photograph of Reconstruction V, missing altogether on another photograph of the same reconstruction, and at position 17 on Reconstructions W, X and Y. It was removed again for study in 1979 (Pl. Xb and c). The roundels in positions 9 and 14 seem to have been lost before the shield entered the Museum, for none has been recorded in those positions. The earliest record, Jobbins's engraving (Cuming 1858: pl. 24, no. 4) shows roundels missing from positions 9, 11, 14 and 17. Roundels 1, 3 and 4 seem to have rotated slightly from their positions on Reconstruction V to Reconstruction W, and roundel 1 was again disturbed judging from the photographs of Reconstruction X. Roundel 27 has a modern rivet, and the empty hole is clearly visible on early photographs. Pieces of 'enamel' seem to have been lost from several of the roundels, and in some instances red sealing-wax has been added.

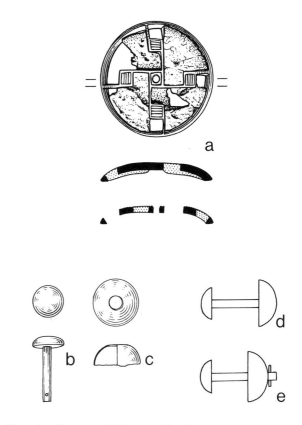

Figure 6. Battersea shield: roundel and rivets: a. the Henry roundel; b. rivet; c. domed washer; d. original arrangement of rivet and washer; e. present arrangement. Scale 2:3.

iii *The Rivets*

The panels were attached to the shield by twenty-four bronze rivets (labelled here a-z, omitting i and o). Some were lost before the shield entered the Museum; not one survives in its original state; and six modern rivets have been added. Each rivet has a shank some 2 mm in diameter and a solid domed head from 6.2 to 7.3 mm across (Fig. 6b). The shank would have passed through the shield and seems to have been secured on the underside by a hollow domed bronze washer (Fig. 6c and d; 9.2 – 10.1 mm across and 3.2 – 4.2 mm high) – seventeen washers survive and seven modern ones have been added. In the course of conservation all the washers have been removed, the shanks drilled, cut and trimmed, and reassembled by fixing a fine steel pin through a new hole drilled near the end of the shank (Fig. 6e). No shank survives to its original length: the longest is now 11.7 mm, which after deducting the height of the domed washer (4 mm) gives a minimum thickness for the shield (including the bronze plating) of 7.7 mm. Detailed study of the shield and all known photographs suggest that the six new rivets and seven washers were made for Reconstruction W (p. 24) and that the rivets and washers were then removed from their original positions and thoroughly muddled.

iv *The Sheets*

Four sheets of thin bronze join, one in each quadrant, to form the background to the face of the shield (two are illustrated, Fig. 7). They are very similar in size, with the following maximum measurements: D, 382 × 173 mm; E, 373 × 172 mm; F, 376 × 170 mm; G, 377 × 170 mm. Their outer border follows the edge of the shield, being overlapped by the rim-binding, and the inner border is cut away more or less to the outline of the decorative panels which just overlap the edge of the sheets. The outlines of the panels are usually quite clear on the face of the sheets, and some of the covered areas are highly polished. The overlap is only slight: in general some 5 mm, but increasing to about 15 mm under the terminals beyond the 'animal horns' on Panels B and C, and even more where there are projecting 'tongues'. In several places the edge of the overlapping panel has worn the sheet, sometimes to the extent of cutting completely through, and some lengths thus cut have been lost. The outer edge has been overlapped for some 3 to 4 mm, and its margin has in places been distorted by the binding-strip. Some of the original surface survives intact – a shiny golden bronze colour with a high polish – but elsewhere there are corroded patches extending to many pinprick perforations and some holes up to 3 mm across. The bronze sheets are 0.2 – 0.3 mm thick, with the exception of Sheet F which is marginally thicker, 0.25 – 0.35 mm, and in better condition.

The edges of the bronze sheets are perforated with holes intended for rivets and pins to secure them to the organic base of the shield. Clearly the holes are not all contemporary, and unfortunately it seems certain that most were made in recent times – since the shield entered the Museum in 1857. The following types can be distinguished: (1) small pin-holes which have not been pre-drilled; (2) drilled 1 mm diameter holes; (3) drilled holes between 1.5 and 2.5 mm in diameter. It seems very likely that the pin-holes are modern: they follow the broken outline rather than the original outline of the sheets (especially the bottom right of Sheet E), and at least one was used for a pin whose head can be seen on a photograph of Reconstruction W (p. 24). The 1 mm diameter drilled holes are modern – Paul Craddock has examined them and is in no doubt that they were made by an electric drill; photographs of Reconstruction W show pins or rivets in these holes, whereas there are no holes in these positions on photographs of the earlier Reconstruction V. The larger drilled holes are probably ancient, although many of them have been re-drilled recently and further distorted by having rivets inserted in slightly different positions on the various reconstructions. No pins, ancient or modern, survived when the shield was dismantled in 1979, and the only rivets are those which passed through the panels and are described in the previous section.

Panels B and C were each attached by seven rivets, and where the rivets made contact with the bronze sheets there are pairs of rivet-holes: the paired holes are ancient in origin (some are now torn or re-drilled) suggesting that the shield could have been once dismantled and reassembled in antiquity. The rivet-holes at the sides of the 'snouts' on Panels B and C (i.e. holes f, g, t and u) survive as pairs; there is no hint of the end-holes (a and x) and it may be that they never penetrated the sheets; and some if not all of the side holes in the circular parts of the panels were secured to the sheets by projecting 'tongues'. Three such tongues survive for Panel B and the fourth (? removed recently) has left a clear impression under the panel. There is only one projecting tongue for Panel C, and no hint of others. The main rivets for Panel A do not penetrate these sheets (though one clipped the edge of Panel C), but there are holes for the pins or rivets which attached the two tags – one in Sheet F is complete but recently re-drilled, and the others are only the edges of holes.

The sheets may have been attached to one another by two pins or rivets in each of the squared ends. The pair of holes in the bottom end of G may be ancient, and there are traces of matching holes in F; the edges of two others survive in the bottom of D, and there is one corresponding hole in E. At the top, of the two holes in this position in D one is probably modern and the other may have been ancient but is now distorted; there are no corresponding holes in G nor any sign of holes in that position in E and F. Marks on the surfaces of the sheets show that D covered E by about 6 mm; F overlapped G by some 5 mm; D may have fitted under the edge of G, but there is no trace of contact between E and F.

The only other ancient holes were used for the binding-strips, which were designed to be attached by rivets only at the top and bottom. Each sheet has several holes in these positions, some torn and re-drilled, and it is now impossible to sort out the original arrangement. Sheet F has two holes (one of them recent) for the attachment of the repair-strip; one corresponding with the hole midway along H3; and one (also in Sheet G) for the rivet at the junction of H3 and 4.

Some of the sheets have been damaged other than by pin- and rivet-holes, tears along the lines of overlaps, corrosion and the loss of tongues. Sheet D was cracked in two, and mended by soldering, at a point some 90 mm from its top corner, and about 90 mm further along the outside edge a curved crack extends 27 mm into the sheet. Sheet E has a semicircular cutting adjoining Panel A: it was masked by a piece of modern copper in Reconstruction W, and judging from the polished border the copper was soldered in position. Photographs of Reconstruction V show a marked fold across the bottom corner and a pronounced dimple – features which were hammered out for Reconstruction W.

v *The Binding-strips*

The edge of the shield was bound by 'U'-section bronze strip. Originally it was in two lengths, each covering one half of the shield divided vertically, but the left half broke and was repaired in antiquity, and later it broke again in two other places.

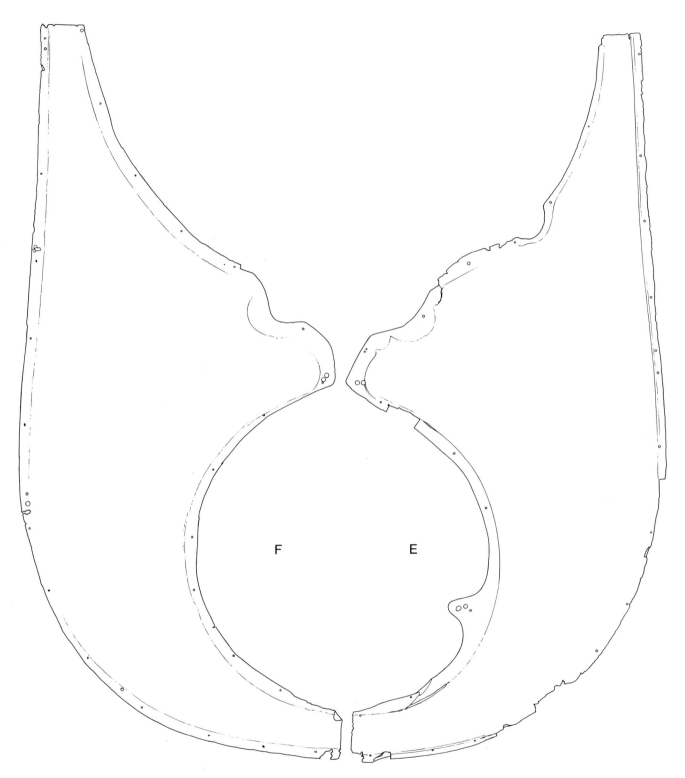

Figure 7. Battersea shield: Sheets E and F. Scale 1:2.

H1 The complete right half is now 769 mm long, measured off the shield with the bronze under no strain. It is about 10 mm deep, binding a thickness of about 7 mm, and some 7 – 7.5 mm wide. It has holes for only two ancient rivets, in the two ends (Fig. 8b and g, d and j), and both positions have been re-drilled in modern times; in addition it has six modern 1 mm pin-holes. Towards the centre it has been under strain and cracked at two points some 7 mm apart on one side and at a corresponding point on the other side; there seems to have been some attempt, in antiquity, to strengthen this area for there are tool-marks on the inside and traces of added bronze on the outside. Obvious file-marks following the curvature of the binding may well have been left for decorative effect. Round the rim, on both sides, is a slight engraved line. The top end of H1 has been shaped, apparently to be covered by another piece of bronze which must have overlapped by up to 6 mm, and some of the shaped area has been cut or torn away (Fig. 8b and g). At this end are two rivet-holes in one face and one in the other, all apparently re-drilled. The bottom end seems also to have been shaped to be overlapped, here for only 2 mm, more than half of which is torn away (Fig. 8d and j). Again there are two rivet-holes in one face (one certainly re-drilled) and one (re-drilled) in the other.

H2 A curved length from the bottom end of the left side binding. It measures 239 mm along the outside. The bottom end, which may have been overlapped by about 1.5 mm, has a rivet-hole which may be ancient (Fig. 8c and k). At the opposite end (Fig. 8e) is a 1.6 mm rivet-hole and a well-defined polished area was covered by the repair-strip HR. About half-way between the two ancient holes is a modern 1 mm pin-hole.

HR The repair-strip, 13 mm long, 11.8 mm deep and 9 mm wide, has an engraved line within each end, and two curved engraved lines across the middle (Fig. 8m). A central (ancient) rivet-hole is 1.5 mm in diameter.

H3 A straight length, 258 mm long (Fig. 8n), has a central ancient rivet-hole 1.6 mm in diameter which has certainly been re-drilled on one side, and half of a similar hole at the top end. There are two modern 1 mm pin-holes, the one at the bottom being within the polished area covered by HR (Fig. 8f). The broken bottom end is slightly distorted, but fits well with the break at the end of H2.

H4 A straight length, 220 mm long, which has separated from H3 along the line of an ancient rivet-hole. There is no rivet-hole at the opposite end, but three modern 1 mm holes along its length.

H5 A curved length from the top end of the left side binding, measuring 271 mm along the outside. It has an ancient rivet-hole (re-drilled) at the top (Fig. 8a and h) and two modern pin-holes. The original end has been shaped, and in part cut or torn away, to take an overlapping piece of bronze (Fig. 8a and h).

The two pieces H2 and H3 fit closely together, although the adjoining edges are worn; certainly the binding-strip was here broken and repaired in antiquity. H3 and H4 have separated at a rivet-hole which may have been contemporary with the repair HR. The break between H4

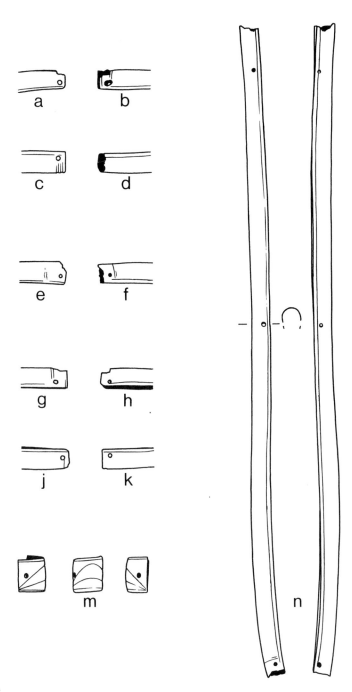

Figure 8. Battersea shield: binding strips. a-f. front: a. H5, top; b. H1, top; c. H2, bottom; d. H1, bottom; e. H2, top; f. H3, bottom. g-k. back: g. H1, top; h. H5, top; j. H1, bottom; k. H2, bottom. m. the repair-strip HR; n. H3 front (left) and back (right). Scale 2:3

and H5 has been distorted, but the details of the two broken edges correspond exactly. It seems likely that at the time of the repair HR, H3/4/5 was in one piece: indeed it may well have been in one piece when the shield was discovered – otherwise it seems unlikely that the piece H4 would have survived.

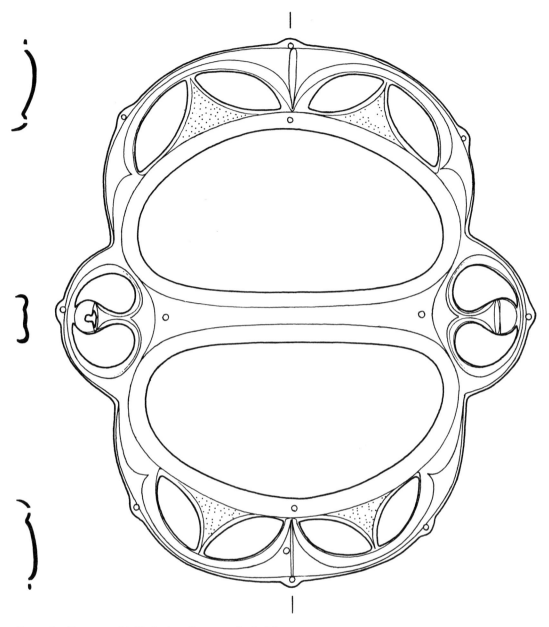

Figure 9. Battersea shield: the handle-cover. Scale 1:1

vi *The Handle-cover*

A delicate object cut and shaped from a thin sheet of bronze (0.6 – 0.8 mm thick), its maximum length is 145.5 mm and its width 131.5 mm (Fig. 9). The central cross-bar is bordered by two oval holes, 82 and 84 mm long and 42 and 43.5 mm wide, whose edges are down-turned about 4 mm deep. At each end of the cross-bar is a repoussé pelta-shape whose swollen stem is encircled to form two comma-shaped holes. On the outsides of the large oval holes are similar repoussé and cut-out forms with punched infilling in the flat triangular shapes. The bronze cover has been attached by pins for which only the holes survive: eight holes in projecting tags, one at each end of the

cross-bar, one in each of the outer borders of the oval holes, and an odd one in the middle of a repoussé motif. It has not been cleaned, and its dark patina gives some idea of the shield's appearance before it was cleaned in the late 1930s.

This object, acquired with the shield and registered as 'probably the covering of the handle of the shield', has never been published although it was included in two theses (Ritchie 1969; Spratling 1972). Technically and stylistically there is no reason to doubt its association with the shield, and in particular the perforated tags may be compared with those on either side of Panel A. No other British La Tène shield has a handle or handle-cover.

La Tène shields were usually provided with wooden handles which crossed horizontally the cavity covered by the boss. This is shown by wooden remains from La Tène itself (Vouga 1923: pl. xvii) and for Britain a similar arrangement is indicated on the model shield from Hod Hill (Smith 1922b: 97-9; now either in private hands or lost) and the leather shield from Clonoura (Pl. XI). La Tène I shields in France had handles of iron secured through to the front of the shield by rivets which often had ornamental heads (e.g. Stead 1968: fig. 17, 1 and 2). Handles from some Hungarian and Swiss shields some-times have elaborate terminals (e.g. Hunyady 1942: pls xii, 19 and 20; xvi, 12; Vouga 1923: pl. xvi, 5 and 6) which superficially resemble Battersea – but the Battersea piece is a cover, not a handle.

The Battersea shield would have had a wooden handle, implied by the pin-holes in the ends of the cover's cross-bar, which could have been grasped comfortably by only a slender hand. It seems very unlikely that such a delicate piece of metalwork, lightly pinned in position, was ever intended to see rough usage.

Reconstructions

In the years since it entered the British Museum the shield has had at least three mounts, and it seems that each time it was removed for conservation or study it was reassembled in a slightly different way. Some of the restoration and repair-work was quite drastic, and it is worth recording its known history in order to distinguish clearly between modern and ancient work. There is no record of the shield's appearance when it was first received in the Museum: no detailed study was then published, and no notes about its reconstruction have survived. However, there is no argument about the arrangement of the major pieces: the three panels and the four background sheets can have fitted only in their present positions and this has always been recognised. But the binding-strips have been arranged in different ways. The strip H1 fits on the right of the shield, but the ends could be reversed. The strips H2 to H5 must be in the correct sequence, but the spacing has been varied. The main doubt relates to the junction of the two halves of binding-strip at top and bottom, where the rivet-holes have been re-drilled and the bronze sheets torn. Depending on the mount, and how tightly the binding-strip clasps the edge of the sheets, there is scope to vary slightly the width of the shield.

Reconstruction V

The first reconstruction seems to have survived from the time of the shield's discovery to the 1930s. It is recorded in an engraving by J.R. Jobbins (Cuming 1858); a coloured lithograph by O. Jewitt (Kemble 1863); a coloured illustration based on a photograph which appeared as the frontispiece to the 1905 edition of the British Museum Early Iron Age guide (Smith 1905); official photographs including an overall view published many times (e.g. Hemp 1928: 279, fig. 12; Vulliamy 1930: pl. v; and even as late as Piggott & Daniel 1951: no. 55); a detail showing Panels A and C which was reproduced in Allen 1904: pl. opp. p. 152; and several photographs taken by or for P. Jacobsthal (including Pl. XII). Vulliamy (1930: 118-19) describes the shield as it then appeared: 'although the front of the bronze is now dull and tarnished, the back is still of a bright golden colour, and we can imagine how brilliant the effect must have been when the front was clean and polished', the handle-cover, which was never cleaned, gives some idea of the patina of the shield at that time.

Judging from a glimpse of apparent woodgrain under the semicircular cutting in Sheet E, the bronze fittings were mounted on a wooden board. Hawkes recalls that this was displayed on a polished mahogany mount with lettering in white, and this is shown on one of Jacobsthal's unpub-lished photographs. There is no evidence that any modern pins or rivets were used in the Victorian reconstruction. The background sheets were crumpled and dented – there is a marked circular 'dimple' on Sheet E; Sheet D was torn in two near the top; and the borders of Panels A and B were slightly battered. The overlaps of the sheets were E over D, F over E, F over G and D over G. As for the rim-binding, it seems that H1 was the opposite way round to the present reconstruction. H2 fitted tightly against H1 and extended beyond the end of Sheet F which would have pulled the repair HR too far down the shield. H3 and H4 in turn were much too far down the shield, and the rivet-hole between them would not have been in line with the corresponding hole in Sheet F. There is a wide gap between H4 and H5, and the top end of H5 fits under the end of H1 and extends well beyond the end of Sheet G.

There were some changes to the roundels in Panel A during the life of this reconstruction. The Jobbins engraving shows three missing roundels (11, 14 and 17) but only one (14) is absent on the illustration published by Smith (1905) Vulliamy (1930), etc. Two of Jacobsthal's photographs show no roundel 14; the Henry Roundel (p. 17) was at position 11; and another now missing (the Missing Roundel p. 17) at position 17. Jacobsthal's overall photograph (Pl. XII) shows the Missing Roundel in position 17 but nothing in position 11.

All the photographs of this reconstruction show rivets missing from positions 1, m, t, w, y and z. The Jobbins engraving shows two missing rivets, but in this respect it is unreliable because it omits some rivet positions (f, g, t and u) and invents others (outside roundels 3 and 23 on Panels B and C).

Reconstruction W

The shield was repaired and re-mounted by H.V. Batten in the late 1930s. A subsequent Research Laboratory report (p. 49) dates this reconstruction and a spectographic analysis carried out at the same time to 1935-6, but there are no original records and it may have been rather later. In a note on the Witham scabbard, Kendrick (1939: 195) refers to this laboratory work 'earlier in the year when the Battersea shield was cleaned'. As the note was published in April 1939, the year to which it refers is almost certainly 1938: Hawkes recalls that Kendrick started his keepership from 1 January 1938 'and his eagerness for metal shining bright was not to be satisfied without its being turned on the Battersea Shield' (letter 17/8/38). This time the shield was mounted on hardboard and the study of several photographs shows that the operation was a drastic one.

The many creases and dents in the background sheets, and in the borders of Panels A and B, and parts of the rim-binding, were removed as completely as possible. The break in the top of Sheet D was repaired with solder, and a piece of thin copper was incorporated to disguise the semicircular cutting in Sheet E. The background sheets were pinned (at least two pinheads are visible on the photographs) and the rim-binding was attached by rivets – operations which created many new perforations in the old metalwork. Three of the sheets were overlapped as before, but E was now put over F instead of the other way round.

The binding strip H1 was the same way round as before, but a gap was left at the bottom between H1 and H2. The repair HR was not in its correct position – part of the polished area of H2 can be seen, so a gap was left between H2 and H3. This gap meant that the original rivet-holes further up H3 and at the junction of H3 and H4 were too high to fit the corresponding holes in Sheet F, but it did allow H4 and H5 almost to touch at the same time as H5 and H1 were touching. The missing rivets in Panels A and C were replaced by modern pins, and only one of the roundels (14) was missing. However, the Henry Roundel was in position 17, mounted at a slightly different angle, and the Missing Roundel, apparently now quite devoid of inlay, was at position 11. Photographs of Reconstruction W have been published by Brailsford (1953: pl. xix, no. 2; 1975a: pl. 25), Megaw (1970: no. 253) and Harding (1974 pls xxx and xxxi). In 1953 the shield was studied in the Research Laboratory but it was not cleaned and not re-mounted.

Reconstruction X

The shield was again dismantled in 1969. It was studied in the Research Laboratory (p. 49) and then mounted on perspex by P.H.T. Shorer. The re-mounting was observed by M.G. Spratling, then carrying out his Ph.D. research, who incorporated notes in his thesis (Spratling 1972). Photographs of this reconstruction were published by Duval (1977: pls. 172 and 223).

At this stage all the modern pins and rivets were removed, apart from those through the decorative panels. The copper strip disguising the semicircular cutting in Sheet E was also removed. The sheets were arranged with overlaps E over D, and F over G, as before; but now G was over D, whilst E and F were just touching. The binding-strip H1 was in the same position as on Reconstructions V and W, and quite a wide gap was left between it and H2. This was the first reconstruction to have H2 to 4 and HR arranged to coincide with the original rivet-holes in the underlying sheets. A wide gap was left between H4 and 5, and H5 was allowed to overlap the end of H1. It was noticed at this time that the Missing Roundel had gone astray.

Reconstruction Y

Following the study of the shield in 1979-80 it was re-mounted on the same perspex base used for Reconstruction X. The relationship between Panels B and C and the four background Sheets D to G cannot be disputed. The impressions of the sheets' tongues on the reverse of the panels leaves no doubt about their sequence. Panel A cannot be reversed: the hole for rivet 1 clips the top of Panel C, whereas rivet-hole h is very slightly further away from the edge and would have missed Panel C if it had been that way round. There was slight overlap between some of the sheets: D certainly overlapped E (the shape of the bottom edge of D is distinctive); E and F meet with no overlap; F clearly overlapped G; G may have overlapped D, and is thus arranged in the present version. F over G is the only overlap employed consistently on all reconstructions.

The position of the left side binding, H2 – 5, is in no doubt because of the rivet-holes used in its repair, and detailed study has shown that H4 undoubtedly once joined H5. But the right side binding could readily be reversed, for it was attached only by a rivet in each end. The problem with regard to the binding is that the two sides do not cover the entire circuit of the shield: there must have been a break at the top and/or the bottom. The circumference could be reduced, in theory, by creating a slight dome to the entire shield, but it seems impossible to support this idea when Panels A – C are quite flat. Because the rivet-holes in the bronze sheets have been re-drilled and torn it is impossible to retrieve the original arrangement with certainty. The position decided upon for the current reconstruction allows the two sides to come close together at the bottom and leaves a marked gap at the top. Two terminals, H5 and the top – as now displayed – of H1, were very clearly overlapped for some length. Reconstruction Y brings these two overlapped terminals together at the top and leaves at the bottom the two terminals (H2 and the bottom of H1) which abutted or had an extremely slight overlap. It assumes a missing cover-strip which must have been at least 16 mm long. As there is no hole in the underlying length of Sheet G, it would seem that there was no central rivet for this cover (unlike HR), which must have been attached by rivets through the holes in the ends of H5 and H1. H1 is thus the opposite way round to all previous reconstructions. It is interesting to see that Franks, in the earliest description of the shield (in Kemble 1863: 190-91) also assumed missing covers: 'the junctions have been originally protected by additional plates with patterns on them, of which only one remains' (the one being HR).

The Henry Roundel was removed during the current study for detailed drawings (Fig. 6a) photographs (Pl. X) and analysis, and was replaced in position 17.

The shield in now 777 mm long; its width across the centre is 341 mm and its maximum width is 359 mm. Reconstruction Y is illustrated in Pl. XIII.

Discussion

i *Previous Studies*

In its first appearance in print the shield was assigned to the correct period – 'this precious example of Celtic art' (Cuming 1858: 330) – and subsequently Franks listed it among his Late Celtic antiquities (in Kemble 1863: 173 and 190-91). Twenty years later it seems to have been given a more precise context in Arthur Evans's Rhind Lectures on Celtic Art, delivered in Edinburgh in December 1895. But the lectures were never published. A summary was issued to those who attended (Leeds 1933: xiii) and this may have been used for the brief accounts published in The Scotsman (cf. Allen 1904: 9, n. 1; 70, n. 4). Smith (1905: 94) quotes the opinion of Evans (presumably given in those lectures) 'that the shield was made within a few years of the birth of Christ'.

J. Romilly Allen (1904: 92-3, and pl. opp. p. 152) extolled the virtues of the Battersea shield: 'perhaps, on the whole, the most beautiful piece of Late-Celtic metalwork that has survived to the present time' in contrast to the Witham shield which he considered 'very inferior' and 'probably of later date' (but he did not suggest an absolute date for either). In the first edition of the British Museum *Guide to the Antiquities of the Early Iron Age*, Reginald Smith devoted very little space to the shield, although he did give it pride of place with a coloured frontispiece. He regarded it as late in a sequence beginning with the Witham shield, 'the embossed portions ... have become more sharp and slender, the pattern more symmetrical and linear, and the coral replaced by red discs of enamel' (Smith 1905: 93-4). He saw the red 'enamel' as significant chronologically – after coral but before the use of other coloured enamels – and thus agreed with the date suggested by Evans. Déchelette (1914: 1174-5) followed Smith's sequence, putting Battersea later than Witham. In the second edition of the *Guide*, also written by Smith (1925), the commentary is similar and the shield retains the frontispiece but with a less sharp reproduction on which the Missing Roundel in position 14 (p. 17) has been crudely coloured.

E.T. Leeds (1933: 11, 23-5, and 25 n. 2) was the first to publish a detailed discussion. Concerned particularly with chronology, he argued against the accepted 'Belgic' date most recently supported by Hawkes (in Kendrick & Hawkes 1932: 205). These are the main points in Leeds's argument: (1) 'The quasi-triangular panels at the base of the enclosed palmettes in the central disk are filled with coils ending in the same leaflets as appear in the decoration of the large Wandsworth-Witham group' (i.e. Pl. IVa). (2) 'The enclosed palmette ... is executed in a manner, in my opinion, quite impossible after the first century BC, and, I should strongly suspect, improbable after the end of the second' (i.e. Fig. 12b). He compared it with motifs on the Clevedon torque and a La Tène I brooch from Hunsbury. (3) The 'key-pattern' shape of the red 'enamel' 'is distinctly rare, except in early work'. Furthermore, applied roundels are more primitive than champlevé enamel. (4) 'The manner in which three of the scrolls are brought together at a solid triangle – is one which is to be encountered commonly and almost exclusively in the second and first centuries BC' (i.e. Pl. IVb). Leeds concluded: 'in short, it adds yet another link with the repertory of La Tène II style (cf. P. Vouga, *La Tène*, Fig. 7k) from which, as already indicated, Celtic ornament in Britain is so largely derived'.

Hawkes was unimpressed: he saw the balanced symmetry of the design as 'the first sign in British art of the approach of Rome' and thought that the Battersea shield 'cannot in fact be other than Belgic' (in Corder & Hawkes 1940: 345 and 343). The point was argued more fully in a review. 'Its central plate displays the *yin-yang* scrolls of the (Belgic) Aylesford bucket: its palmettes recall the bucket's handle-attachments: its clay-backed cloisonné enamel reappears in the (Belgic) Lexden tumulus, and the key-pattern of the cloisons is just that characteristic of the catch-plates of Late La Tène brooches. And for explanation of the even purity of its swinging curves, so unlike much late British design, can we not adduce the influence of classical Augustan metalwork, as seen for instance on some of the Bosco Reale and Hildesheim silver (*Piot*, pls ix, x, xxi (2, 3), xxv: *Hildesheimer Silberfund*, pls xxiv, xxxii – iii)? Such Augustan influence should belong to the turn of the first centuries, being thereafter swamped in the degenerate Celticism evident at Santon Downham and Westhall' (Hawkes 1933: 153).

Jacobsthal examined the Battersea shield in the 1930s, and left a short typescript catalogue-entry (copy in the Department of Prehistoric & Romano-British Antiquities, British Museum). His promised paper on 'Celtic Art in the British Islands' (cf. Jacobsthal 1935: 127) did not appear and his monograph on the British material, already 'eagerly awaited' in 1951 (Fox 1951: 187) now to be published with Jope, is still awaited. The Jacobsthal typescript refers very briefly to features of Augustan character (cf Hildesheim) – the same point made by Hawkes (above) and followed by de Navarro (1952: 80-81): 'a feature of the ornament of the shield has been compared with a similar feature found on Roman silver-work of the time of Augustus, and thus dates the shield at roughly about the time of our Lord's birth'.

An even later date was proposed by Kendrick (1938: 11-12) who saw it 'as an example of the elegant semi-classicism of the native style in the Belgic east about the time of the Claudian invasion'. The 'symmetrical curvilinear pattern ... seems ... to approach the style of Roman volutes and the pelta-type and lotus-flower arrangement of scrolls'. 'But it is a very much altered scroll, very prim, arid, and leafless'. Stylistically later than Witham, 'the one is taut and dynamically vigorous; the other soft, spreading and weak'.

At the international meeting of the congress of Prehistoric and Protohistoric Sciences, at Madrid in 1954, Brailsford presented the results of recent laboratory work and looked briefly at the chronology of the Battersea shield. Whilst appreciating the arguments for a late date he was also influenced by Piggott's remarks on the Wandsworth round boss: 'there are a series of symmetrical arrangements of patterns owing nothing to reimposed ideas of classical "fold-over" designs, but original to Celtic art in Britain as on the Continent' (Atkinson & Piggott 1955: 216). He concluded cautiously that the 'arguments for an early date put forward by Leeds cannot be lightly dismissed' (Brailsford 1956: 760).

Sir Cyril Fox (1958: 27 – 9) threw caution to the winds, and confidently proclaimed: 'its date will be about 75 BC'. Having declared this conclusion, based entirely on the 'fold-over symmetry', he explored details of the decoration and found many traditional features: 'Apart from its symmetry, and certain refinements which establish its uniqueness ... very little is brought into the pattern that is not, on the evidence of other work, already part of the Gallo-British tradition. The scrolls incorporating hollow-sided "triangles" are related to those on Gallic helmets (e.g. Amfreville, Jacobsthal, *Plate 78*) and seen also in many British works; the "closed" palmettes from which they emerge are also traditional (Figure 82, A4, B9, 10); the snaily coils, comma forms, and leaf terminals associated with these are seen on the Torrs horns and cap, the paired coils on the axes of the lesser circles are based on the lateral features of the decoration of the Witham shield-boss: and so on'. 'The most remarkable and novel details, perhaps, are those which enliven the narrow bands in high relief which adorn the two lesser circles', details which he derived from the repoussé work on the Wandsworth shield-boss. Fox also drew attention to the 'nose-like structure' ('animal-head') and its counterpart on the Witham shield; and pointed to the similarity between the swastikas on the roundels and that on the Llyn Cerrig horn-cap. Although he saw links with the Witham shield and more particularly with the Wandsworth round boss he felt that it was 'difficult, however, to justify an earlier date than c. 75 BC for so formal a piece' – the Battersea shield followed the others *after a considerable gap*' (his italics).

Jope (1961a: 81 – 2) followed the accepted sequence – 'at the end of the series, the Battersea shield' – but without the long gap required by Fox: 'certain affinities of the design to those of the Witham and Wandsworth-roundel shields make it difficult to place this much more than a generation after them – 150 BC seems a reasonable limit'.

Powell (1966: 236) settled for a position midway between Fox and Jope, recording that 'recent estimations ... place it about the turn of the second and first centuries BC'. But a few years later Piggott (1970: introduction, and nos 13, 14 and 31) dated the Witham-Wandsworth bronzes to the first century BC, and Jope (1971: 68, n. 39) sharply cut his date for the Battersea shield, referring to the Wandsworth round boss as 'the central unit from a shield of Battersea type (with its strong Augustan flavour). This Wandsworth roundel again probably has a poor copy of the relief wavy-line technique of Witham and the Wandsworth mask shield, and with its sense of perspective – the oblique view of a bird rising from the water (pl. xxv) – seems to follow sliver-ware of Augustan age'. A few years later Jope still regarded the Battersea shield and the Wandsworth round boss as 'fine works of the late first century BC or earlier first century AD'. (1976: 176; cf. also 1978: 33-4).

Megaw (1970: 150 – 51) whilst admitting a general similarity with the Witham shield, emphasised late features and especially Roman influence. 'The dotted background is a feature of much of later British metal-work'; the relief ornament he considered 'to be made by press-moulding, a technique followed by a late group of so-called "casket ornament" strips'; 'the whole shield, with its markedly waisted form, owes more to Roman military equipment as seen, for example, on Trajan's Column and to provincial bronzes of the Augustan period'; 'even the employment of variants on the trumpet spiral on the Battersea shield have perfectly good analogies amongst provincial Roman material'. The use of red 'enamel' he compared with objects from 'Belgic graves of the first century AD', and the swastika motif with that on the Llyn Cerrig Bach horn-cap. He drew attention to the La Tène III sword-scabbard 'from the same reach of the Thames', and concluded that the shield was 'a late piece made under strong Roman influence'.

The 1969 reconstruction (Reconstruction X) was observed by (and indeed influenced by) Spratling who was thus able to handle the component pieces of the shield. That work is recorded in his unpublished thesis (Spratling 1972: 170, 184-6, 527-9) along with a detailed description and some pertinent comments. He emphasised that the circular shield-boss was a Late La Tène innovation on the Continent, and suggested that the three bosses from the Polden Hill hoard could have been mounted in the same way as at Battersea. The Wandsworth roundel could have belonged to a similar shield and the type may be represented by one of the mini-shields from Worth. Spratling followed Smith in deriving this arrangement of three roundels from spined shields with terminal roundels, such as that from the Witham – although not all shields of Battersea type need be later than shields with spines. Indeed, he noted a marked roundness of the bosses on the Witham shield and the Wandsworth mask shield and wondered if they too could have been influenced by the Late La Tène hemispherical boss. Neither Witham nor Battersea types of shield could be matched on the Continent but 'it does seem possible that there may have been ceremonial shields of similar design to (Battersea) in the Classical world, for ... the outline of this shield is paralleled by the ceremonial *ancilia* of the Salian priests at Rome ... [and] ... the scroll ornament around the circular boss on a ceremonial shield (of a different outline) depicted on the late first century BC monument to Caecilia Metella on the Appian Way ... (Fig. 214B) bears a striking resemblance to the layout of the ornament on the central roundel' (ibid.: 186).

In the most recent publication of the shield, Brailsford (1975a: 25 – 6) reiterated the late date, being influenced in particular by the comparison of the red 'enamel' roundels with those from Hertford Heath and Lexden, and the 'almost mechanical quality of precision' of the repoussé – 'one expects the Battersea shield to come very late in the sequence of Early Celtic art in Britain'.

ii *Early Celtic Art in Britain*

The sequence of Early Celtic Art in Britain relies on stylistic and typological factors founded on some tenuous Continental parallels, for there are few associated finds. Continental archaeologists have the advantage of being able to base their studies on Jacobsthal's great work on *Early Celtic Art* (1944) – still fundamental in spite of modifications and expansions made by subsequent scholars. But for Britain the great man left little in print, and he must be interpreted through brief references mainly in de Navarro's publications. It may be that de Navarro read Jacobsthal's paper on 'Celtic Art in the British Islands' – certainly he had seen at least one unpublished paper (de Navarro 1943: 393-4; 1966: 150; 1972: 294, n. 3). It seems that for Britain Jacobsthal numbered his art styles, starting with the Continental I (Early), II (Waldalgesheim) and III (Sword and Plastic sub-styles) – and then IV, the Insular Style.

Style II 'is the earliest La Tène style to reach Britain, but it is very sparsely represented here; an excellent example is the horn-cap for a chariot found in the Thames at Brentford' (de Navarro 1952: 73, ? following Jacobsthal). Jacobsthal (1944: 154) ascribed the Cerrig-y-Drudion 'bowl' to this style, as well as the ornament on the Newnham Croft bracelet and Beckley brooch (in Hawkes & Jacobsthal 1945: 123). Style III 'almost, but not quite, unknown in Britain ... is none the less highly important for the British Isles, for out of it was evolved the first La Tène art of these islands, termed by Jacobsthal Style IV' (de Navarro 1952: 75; but Jope, in a letter, comments that Jacobsthal disapproved of the term 'Style IV'). Subsequently called by de Navarro the 'Early Insular Style' Style IV included the Wandsworth bosses and Witham shield, the Torrs chamfrein and other pieces first grouped by Leeds (1933: 6-15). The only other style recognised by de Navarro (1952: 78) is the 'Mirror Style'.

In the discussion following their detailed study of the Torrs chamfrein, Atkinson & Piggott (1955) preferred to re-group the British pieces, and abandon the numbered styles. They recognised an 'Early School' or 'Torrs-Wandsworth Style', sub-divided into an earlier phase (Newnham-Torrs, including some Style II pieces and Torrs) and a later phase (Witham-Wandsworth, comprising the rest of Style IV). More or less contemporary with the beginnings of this 'Early School' they recognised a different group (Cerrig-y-Drudion, Wisbech and Standlake), and to an earlier stage they assigned most of the Thames daggers and the first La Tène I brooches in Britain (ibid.: 228-31).

The numbered styles played little part in Fox's survey of British Celtic art (1958). They are mentioned briefly (ibid.: 5 and 19), but he was more concerned to identify schools and workshops. Style IV was vaguely defined as 'our British Iron "B" art' (ibid.), and the Mirror Style (ibid.: 84 ff.) was a development whose ancestry was traced via the Llyn Cerrig shield-boss to the Meare and Amerden scabbards on the one hand and the Llyn Cerrig plaque, Grimthorpe disc and Ulceby horse-bit on the other (ibid.: 32-45; cf. also Fox 1946: 48-56).

Subsequent writers on British Celtic art have not returned to the numbered styles, and the only form of classification in general use is that of the named styles used by Jacobsthal on the Continent (e.g. Jope 1961a; Frey & Megaw 1976; Megaw 1983). An alternative scheme was proposed by Duval (1971 – a lecture delivered in 1966) who criticised Jacobsthal's classification because it was incomplete, dealing only with the earlier material, and composed of a heterogeneous collection of named styles derived from chronology (Early), topography (Waldalgesheim), artefact (Sword) and morphology (Plastic). He proposed a more rational scheme for Celtic art both Continental and Insular, rejected a sequence of numbered styles, and suggested an 'Early Strict Style' followed by 'Free Graphic Style' (corresponding to Waldalgesheim and including Brentford and the Torrs Horns), 'Free Plastic Style' (including the Torrs cap, Wandsworth boss and Llyn Cerrig plaque), and then 'Late Strict Style' (with the Battersea shield, as well as the Llyn Cerrig boss, Bugthorpe scabbard, Snettisham bracelet, the Mirrors, and Elmswell plaque). But Duval's new approach has failed to gain widespread acceptance either on the Continent or in Britain. For Britain there is some value in having a classification related to but not identical with the Continental scheme, and it is proposed here to return to the Jacobsthal/de Navarro numbered styles, using the definitions quoted above. In addition to de Navarro's summaries it should be noted that Style I does exist in Britain (cf. Jope 1961a: 73). In order to complete the sequence it will be adequate for the present purposes to define as Style V the tradition studied in particular by Sir Cyril Fox, with designs engraved/chased or constructed from relief lobes, often with hatched backgrounds and featuring distinctively-shaped voids (Fox 1946: 46-58).

The sequence of art-styles may be subjected to some form of control by considering two types of artefact, brooches and scabbards, which can be arranged in independent typological sequences covering the length of the La Tène period. Both types are sometimes decorated, which relates them to the art-styles, and there are a few brooches with useful associations.

The earliest La Tène brooches in Britain are related to

the 'Marzabotto' form which on the Continent belongs to the end of the fifth century (Hodson 1964: 137; Kruta 1979: 82). Several were Insular products, employing distinctive British hinge mechanisms, and a few are usefully decorated. A 'Marzabotto' brooch from Wood Eaton, Islip (Fox 1927: 76, fig. 7) has ring and dot ornament on the foot and on the sides of the bow – where the rings are linked by pairs of diagonal lines to form a design of two scrolls separated by criss-cross lines which may well be derived from the Early Style (cf. especially Kruta 1977: fig. 1, no. 1; Schwappach 1969: fig. 6, no. 56 – 'Metal Style' ornament on Armorican pottery). A brooch of similar form from Hammersmith (Fox 1927: 82, fig. 13; but the decoration first noticed by Wardman 1972: no. 99) has worn ornament terminating in derived palmettes in a frame (closely comparable to Schwappach 1969: fig. 2, no. 4 and fig. 6, no. 60 – more examples of 'Metal Style' ornament on Armorican pottery); and another from Hunsbury (Fox 1927: 83, fig. 16; for the decoration see Leeds 1933: 23, fig. 8 and Jacobsthal 1944: pl. 274, P. 378) has a series of heart-like 'palmettes' on the bow. The decoration on a 'Marzabotto' brooch from Box (Fox 1927: 82, fig. 14, but for the detail see Hawkes 1976a: 9, fig. 5d) is an S-motif – a recurring theme in Early Style art (e.g. Jacobsthal 1944: no. 171).

Perhaps a brooch from Maiden Castle (Fox 1927: 93, fig. 25) had Style II ornament, but it is badly worn and difficult to interpret. Jacobsthal (in Hawkes & Jacobsthal 1945: 123) thought that it might be 'a dishevelled copy' of the ornament on brooches such as one from Münsingen (i.e. Hodson 1968: t. 49, no. 799). However, the Maiden Castle brooch is some remove from a 'Marzabotto' and even features the foot attached to the bow in a way which was not common on the Continent until La Tène III. But there are other La Tène I brooches with foot and bow cast together, both in Britain and on the Continent (Stead 1981: pl. 36, showing British and Continental pieces together). The point is important, because amongst the coral-ornamented brooches of this type is one from Newnham Croft associated with a bracelet with Style II decoration (Fox 1958: 10, fig. 6). The foot of the Newnham Croft brooch turns back at a sharp angle (with a slightly upturned catch-plate) and has a moulded collar at the junction of foot and bow, factors which suggest La Tène II influence (for the shape of the foot cf. La Tène II brooches from Wandsworth, Cotton 1979, and Wetwang Slack, Dent 1982: fig. 4, burial 160). Furthermore, the 'snail-shell' under the catch-plate has been classified by Jacobsthal as a 'Plastic Style' (Style III) feature (Hawkes & Jacobsthal 1945: 123).

The typical sequence from the 'Marzabotto' brooch saw the arched bow gradually lowered and lengthened. Some of the brooches with the longest flat bows show clear La Tène II influence in having a marked collar at the junction of foot and bow. One such from Sawdon (Stead 1979: 66, fig. 24, no. 2) also carries an excellent example of the tightly-coiled spirals typical of Style IV.

The typological sequence of brooches from those with long flat bow through long and slightly involuted to short

and markedly involuted bow has now been neatly confirmed by stratificiation in the Wetwang Slack cemetery (Dent 1982: 439-44). It is unfortunate that most of the Yorkshire brooches are made of iron, because only bronze examples carry useful decoration. Of the long and slightly involuted brooches a fine bronze example from Danes Graves (Stead 1979: 69-70 fig. 26, no. 1) has cast lobe ornament under the bow and carved inlay ornament on the top. The arrangement on the bow recalls the 'S' on the Box brooch, but in higher relief and terminating at one end in a 'Plastic Style' 'snail-shell' (Hawkes & Jacobsthal 1945: 123). Of the shorter involuted brooches some are moulded in the same tradition, but two from Oxfordshire have rather different decoration on broad flat foot-plates. 'The ornament on the involuted brooch from Beckley, a "loop flanked by whirligigs", is one of the stock patterns of the Waldalgesheim Style' (ibid.). The decoration on the Beckley brooch is very worn; Jacobsthal approved of the interpretive drawing given by Savory 1939; 260, fig. 17c, but not the version first published by Evans 1915: 271, fig. 2; different drawings have since appeared in Fox 1958: 13, fig. 9 and Harding 1974: 188, fig. 64a. Another brooch of this type was found in 1952 on the Wood Eaton site at Islip (ibid. fig. 64b, cf. Case & Kirk 1952: 217, fig. 41); its decoration, somewhat similar but much better preserved, resembles the same parallel quoted by Jacobsthal for the Beckley decoration (i.e. Jacobsthal 1944: pl. 277, P. 443).

La Tène III brooches only rarely carry the sort of decoration that can be correlated with other finds. In the main they are fairly closely linked to Continental traditions and are not usefully decorated. From the end of the first century BC Roman influence is strong, but Celtic designs are still found, especially on the elaborately decorated gilt-bronze brooches from Carmarthen (Boon & Savory 1975) and Great Chesters (Charlesworth 1973). The latter, the Aesica brooch, whose symmetrical cast scrolls may be compared with the designs on the Elmswell plaque (Corder & Hawkes 1940) and the Meyrick helmet (Brailsford 1975a: 40-43), is a version of the thistle brooch probably dating from the second half of the first century AD but apparently not buried until two centuries later.

For the later stages of British Celtic art there are some interesting associations between brooches and other artefacts. Unfortunately the two brooches found with decorated mirrors (Smith 1909a; Spratling 1970a: 13-15) cannot be closely dated. The one, with the St Keverne mirror, lacks the catch-plate and most of the spring so that it cannot be classified. The other, with the Birdlip mirror, is a distinctive type descended from the Aylesford brooch and presumably dating before the Roman Conquest (there is a rather similar one from a pre-Conquest level at Dragonby: the two are illustrated together, Boon & Savory 1975: fig. 2, nos 2 and 3, who also refer to the stratification of the Dragonby brooch, p. 44, n. 7). More useful are the brooches from the Polden Hill and Santon Downham hoards. From Santon Downham there were no fewer than nine brooches: five were thistle brooches (Smith 1909b: 159, figs 9 and 10) and the other four were Colchester-derivatives. Polden Hill produced the head of a Colchester brooch, two Colchester-derivatives (both with reversed hooks) and three penannular brooches (Brailsford 1975b: 228-9, fig. 6). The thistle brooch belongs to the first century AD (Ettlinger 1973: type 24, 10 BC – AD 70) but more significantly it seems that Colchester-derivatives appeared only just before the Roman conquest (Mackreth 1981: 138). On these grounds neither the Polden Hill nor Santon Downham hoards can be dated any earlier than c. AD 40. Quite apart from the brooches the two hoards have other features in common, such as the harness mounts with red champlevé enamel (still with features of Style V ornament, Brailsford 1975b: pls xxiia and xxiiia; Smith 1909b: fig. 1) and the fragmentary horse-bit from Santon Downham (ibid. fig. 6) belonging to the type well-represented at Polden Hill (Brailsford 1975b: figs 2 and 3). Red enamelled harness fittings also occur in the Westhall hoard (e.g. Leeds 1933: coloured plate I, no. 6) which like Santon Downham was found in a cauldron, and both hoards include discs similarly decorated with animals (Smith 1909b: fig. 7; Smith 1925: fig. 168). There seems to be no sound evidence for dating any champlevé enamel in Britain earlier than the horizon of these hoards (but note also that coral was still being used, Brailsford 1975b: 230, pl. xxiiib; and see p.34 for possible enamel on the Brentford 'horn-cap'). The Santon Downham hoard also produced a piece of 'casket' ornament noted by Hawkes in the full discussion of the type (in Corder & Hawkes 1940: 346, fig. 2) which he dates around the middle of the first century AD.

For the present purposes decorated scabbards are more useful and several important pieces have been discovered recently. A weapon from Orton Meadows (Stead 1984) can lay some claim to being the earliest La Tène long-sword from Britain. Its chape has an open end (Fig. 10a), typical of La Tène I, but beyond that it is bridged on both sides unlike most La Tène scabbards which are bridged on the back and clamped on the front. This feature may be compared with some particularly early La Tène I scabbards, including that from the Somme-Bionne cart-burial associated with a Greek cup manufactured about 420 BC; but it also occurs, and the chape-end can be closely matched, on the later Standlake scabbard (see below). The Orton Meadows scabbard is decorated with geometric ornament including compass-drawn arcs which play an important part in the continental 'Early Style' (Jacobsthal 1944: pls 261-4; Schwappach 1969, 1973; Lenerz-de Wilde 1977). In particular arcs bordered by dots like this may be compared with Jacobsthal 1944: pl. 261, P. 4, and Schwappach 1973: fig. 10. There is similar compass-drawn ornament on the dagger-sheath from Minster Ditch (Jope 1961b: no. 14, and p. 316) whose tubular chape is a Late Hallstatt form, and also on the borders of dagger-sheaths with La Tène I chapes. The arcs on a sheath from Hammersmith (ibid.: no. 18) were figured by Jacobsthal (1944: pl. 264, no. 68), and another from the same part of the Thames (Jope 1961b: no. 23, pl. xxi, E) has interlocking arcs with dotted infilling like Schwappach 1973: figs 5, no. 6; 6, nos 2 and 5. A dagger-sheath from Wandsworth (Jope 1961b: no. 19) has

a curious oval chape cast with ornament which may be compared with that on the Wood Eaton 'Marzabotto' brooch. Others in this series of Late Hallstatt and La Tène I dagger-sheaths have lines of triangular or criss-cross ornament similar to that on the Orton Meadows scabbard (ibid.: nos 16, 19, 21 and 24), which provide a link with the remains of a sheath (or scabbard) from Wisbech (ibid.: pl. xxiv). The dominant motif on the Wisbech piece is two confronted scrolls of interlocking S-forms – lyres which are derived from lotus petals flanking palmettes (Fox 1958: fig. 54). It recalls the design on the Cerrig-y-Drudion 'bowl' and its ancestry may be traced via Brittany (for the Wisbech palmette see Schwappach 1969: fig. 6, no. 60) to the Early Style art in Champagne.

Apart from Orton Meadows only one other decorated English scabbard with an open chape-end has been published, and that was found in the Thames near Standlake (Fig. 10b; Piggott 1950: 4, pl. ii; Jope 1961a; 76, pl. va and c; note that this chape too is bridged on both sides). It has two panels of decoration: at the top, in repoussé, what seems to be a palmette-derivative (ibid.) bounded by a motif similar to that in the lower panel – a wave-tendril design typical of Style II (de Navarro 1959: 91, n. 25, suggesting that the two panels were not contemporary; 1972: 275; for the design in the lower panel cf. a Hungarian scabbard of La Tène I type, Szabo 1977: fig. 3).

The lack of chape-ends has hindered the identification of British La Tène I scabbards but there are several swords of La Tène I shape, especially from the Thames, and two of them are in the remains of scabbards with distinctive dragon-pair ornament (Stead 1984). This oriental-looking motif was certainly in use before the end of La Tène I, and the British examples are relatively early in the sequence. A Hungarian origin was suggested by de Navarro (1959: 103; 1972: 230), but subsequent discoveries have considerably increased the numbers found in the West (cf. especially Bulard 1979). Certainly de Navarro was right to exclude this device from the Swiss Sword Style (Style III) because it is too widespread – 'the motif is best regarded as an inter-Celtic "currency"' (de Navarro 1972: 237). The Thames dragon-pairs are important because they demonstrate close contacts with the Continent, apparently in the first half of the third century BC, and they introduce a motif which inspired designs in Styles IV and V.

In particular the design on the iron scabbard from Fovant (Stead 1984) is obviously derived from a dragon-pair, and it incorporates the tightly-coiled spirals typical of Style IV. Quite apart from the spirals, the shapes and shadings of the Fovant motifs may be compared with those on some of the decorated bronze scabbards from Northern Ireland – especially one from the Bann now on loan to the British Museum (Raftery 1983: no. 270). The Fovant blade is of La Tène I length, but not typical in shape; its chape-end could be regarded as typologically transitional between I and II, for there is a very slight gap between chape-end and scabbard-plates (Fig. 10c). Although there is no surviving chape with the Bann scabbard-plate, those on other decorated (Style IV) scabbards in the area, and

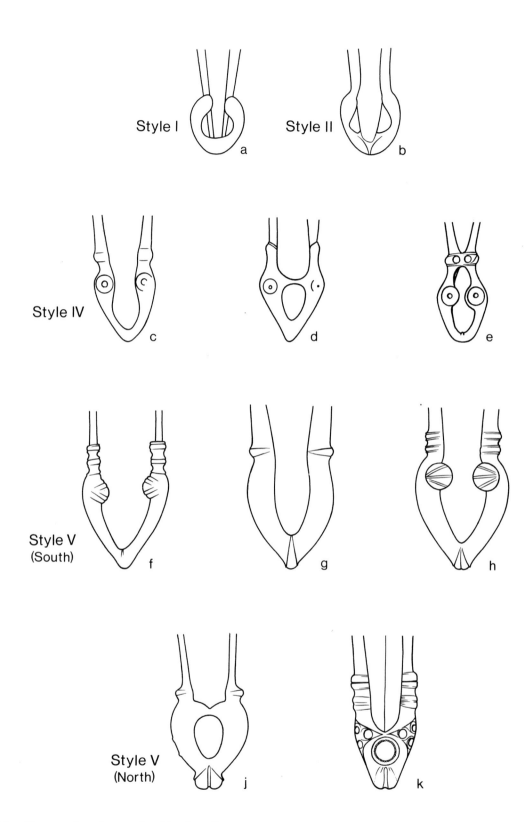

Figure 10. Chape-ends on decorated scabbards: a. Orton Meadows; b. Standlake; c. Fovant; d. Little Wittenham (1961); e. Athenry, Co. Galway, Eire; f. Henley; g. Little Wittenham (1982); h. Hunsbury; j. Bugthorpe; k. Grimthorpe.

indeed the only chapes known from Northern Ireland, are La Tène I in type (Fig. 10e; Jope 1954: 87-8; fig. I, right; pl. vii, right; Raftery 1983: figs 110-12).

When first published there was a chape-end attached to the sword from the River Witham now in the Duke of Northumberland's collection (Willson 1852) but unfortunately it has since been lost. Its scabbard survives only in the form of a repoussé bronze panel which once adorned its mouth – a point of comparison with the Standlake scabbard, but the art-style represented here is very different. The repoussé design is reflected in the engraved motifs which adorn it to create a masterpiece of Style IV – that 'insular phenomenon – perhaps the most magnificent and certainly the most individual artistic contribution of the La Tène civilisation' (de Navarro 1943: 393–4). Details of the engraving and even the diagonal alignment of the design point to influence from the Hungarian Sword Style (Style III). Jacobsthal once regarded the Witham sword as late – some two to three hundred years later than Hungarian examples (Jacobsthal 1939: 28), just as he had seen Roman influence in the Witham shield (de Navarro 1943: 394), although later he favoured a much earlier date 'very soon after 250 BC' (de Navarro 1966: 150).

A bronze chape found at Little Wittenham in 1961 (Harding 1972: 173, pl. 79D) has a terminal not dissimilar from the Fovant chape-end (Fig. 10d). Decoration occupies the central part of the chape, like the lower panel on the Standlake scabbard, but differs in that the basic shape is 'cut-out'. The decoration is on the back of the chape, in a position curious from a visual point of view but logical functionally because the back is the solid piece wrapped round and clamped to the front. Although it does not feature tightly-coiled spirals, the design may be compared with both the Bann and Fovant pieces especially in the way in which the deep central parts of the shapes are occupied by circles (ovals on the Bann and Fovant scabbards) bordered by hatching. Resemblances with the Sutton scabbard-plate (Fox 1958: pl. 21) suggest that it too was a Style IV piece (cf. de Navarro 1966: 148-50).

A fine scabbard from Henley (Rutland 1972) sheaths a sword much longer than the Little Wittenham blade, but there is an interesting comparison between the two scabbards because Henley too has a panel of 'cut-out' ornament on the back of the chape. The Henley scabbard is a complex piece, whose worn decoration at the top should perhaps be classified as Style IV, whilst the 'cut-out' ornament on the chape is undoubtedly Style V – related to the design on the Llyn Cerrig Bach plaque. The chape has certainly been repaired, and it is possible (but by no means certain) that the scabbard originally had a different chape.

The change from Style IV to V seems to coincide with an increase in the length of the sword in southern England. Later swords in the south have blades ranging up to almost 900 mm long, but in the north the situation is very different and only rarely is the length of a La Tène I blade exceeded; most Iron Age swords north of the Humber vary from 400 to 600 mm long. The long North Grimston sword (blade more than 740 mm long) is an obvious stranger in

Yorkshire and it is interesting to note that it was found with a short sword with anthropoid hilt which some scholars have regarded as an import (e.g. Hawkes, in Clarke & Hawkes 1955: 211). In Yorkshire there are two decorated bronze scabbards (unlike most of those in the south they have iron back-plates) – Grimthorpe, which is associated with a disc convincingly linked to Style V pieces by Fox (1958: 33-5) and Bugthorpe which has fine engraved Style V ornament (ibid.: 41); for the chape-ends see Fig. 10j and k.

The Henley chape-end (Fig. 10f), a heavy cast piece with terminal lip-motif typologically much more advanced than the 1961 Little Wittenham chape-end, and its imitation chape-clamps which are independently riveted onto the scabbard-plate (but apparently secondary on this Henley scabbard) are features which link it with another group of scabbards from Hunsbury, Meare and one found at Little Wittenham in 1982 (Piggott 1950: 6-10, fig. 3, nos 1 and 3; Sherratt 1983). These three scabbards share other features – a decorative panel at the top and a pronounced mid-rib; Hunsbury (? with the memory of a dragon-pair) and Meare carry Style V engraved and cast ornament with hatched backgrounds, and Little Wittenham (1982) has similar cast ornament (worked in wax for a *cire perdue* finished product) and a panel of elaborate repoussé which recalls the Style V Llyn Cerrig plaque. The chape-ends from Hunsbury and Little Wittenham (1982) are illustrated in Fig. 10h and g.

The long lower loop-plate on the Meare scabbard is a La Tène III feature shared with related scabbards from London (Smith 1925: pl. ix, no. 4) and Lakenheath (Piggott 1950: fig. 3 – a false lower loop-plate as Isleham, below) both of which have laddered chapes – a distinctive La Tène III feature matched on the Amerden scabbard whose mouth bears Style V decoration (ibid. fig. 3, no. 4).

Finally, another group of three La Tène III bronze scabbards, with straight mouth, full length non-functional extension to the lower loop-plate and broad rounded tip, is firmly linked with Style V by the decoration on the Isleham example (Stead et al. 1981).

The sequence established by relating art-styles to brooches and scabbards may be illustrated in diagrammatic form (Table II). The typology of the scabbards corresponds well with the sequence of art-styles, and so do the La Tène I brooches. However, La Tène II brooches present a problem, for the typologically late Beckley and Wood Eaton involuted brooches have ornament which has been classified as the relatively early Style II. Forty years ago it was possible to conclude that they 'will have been made when the Waldalgesheim Style was still in existence, but side by side with the new Plastic Style; in other words on the verge of La Tène I and II, somewhere late in the second quarter of the third century BC' (Hawkes & Jacobsthal 1945: 124). But the Wetwang Slack stratification shows that the first involuted brooches developed after the appearance of La Tène II influences, and suggests that brooches of Beckley type are late in the sequence. Only one brooch from the Wetwang Slack cemetery has been interpreted as La Tène III, and that occupies a late position in the cemetery (Barrow 117, later by stratification than 115 which had a brooch of Beckley type with hints of decoration). It is a curious brooch, without close parallel: the long flat bow suggests a position much earlier in the Yorkshire sequence; but the two-coiled spring with external chord cannot be matched from the other Yorkshire burials although it is a feature of some La Tène III brooches in southern England (Stead 1976: fig. 1, no. 3; fig. 2, no. 6; fig. 3, no. 3; fig. 4, no. 2); and the solid catch-plate, although not common in La Tène III, features on the latest brooch (of different type) from the Burton Fleming cemetery (Stead 1979: fig. 26, no. 6). Dent's interpretation of the stratification seems reasonable, but it implies that brooches of Beckley type date at least a century later than Jacobsthal suggested (Dent 1982: especially p. 446). The only other stratified sequence of these brooches, from Croft Ambery, is unhelpful with long flat bow, long involuted and short involuted all in the same phase (Stanford 1974: 162-5). If the ornament on the Beckley and Wood Eaton brooches has been correctly classified, then it would seem that in some areas Style II ornament was used, at least on minor objects, throughout the currency of Style IV.

Table II also relates British art styles in a very general way to the Continental La Tène periods. Style I ornament was used on both brooches and sheaths/scabbards at an early stage in La Tène I: it could well have been in use in England before the end of the fifth century BC. Compass-drawn and other geometric motifs, as well as palmettes, lyres and S-motifs, suggest links with an important centre of Early Style art in Champagne. There, alone of Continental La Tène provinces, a close connection between the Early and Waldalgesheim Styles can be demonstrated (Frey 1976: 148), a connection which causes confusion when it comes to classifying works derived from that tradition. Thus the Cerrig-y-Drudion 'bowl' was classified as Waldalgesheim by Jacobsthal (1944: 154) followed by Jope (1961a: 74) who included with it the Wisbech scabbard-plate. Hawkes (1976b: 165) prefers to distinguish such pieces from 'true Waldalgesheim derivatives' like the Newnham Croft bracelet and Brentford 'horn-cap'. The difficulty here is that in Britain too there is continuity between Styles I and II. The design on the Cerrig-y-Drudion 'bowl' may be compared with that on the Canosa helmet which seems to be dated to the late fourth century BC (Frey 1974: 150; Frey & Megaw 1976: 54; but Kruta 1978: 422 would put it in the middle of the fourth century) and belongs to the stage at which the Waldalgesheim Style was developing. On the Continent the Waldalgesheim Style is now seen to owe more to contact with classical art in north Italy than to the genius of the Waldalgesheim Master (e.g. Kruta 1974; 1982).

For the genesis of Style IV the significance of the Cernon-sur-Coole scabbard has often been quoted (Leeds 1933: 8; de Navarro 1952: 73-4; but see Megaw 1973; 131) if only because it is much nearer to England than other examples of 'Sword Style' engraved art. But it is a particularly significant piece because it also has Waldalgesheim Style art on the suspension loop-plates, and

the date suggested by de Navarro (1972: 295, n. 2) – early in La Tène II – is as early as any example of Style IV can yet be placed. In terms of absolute chronology, it is worth recalling that dendrochronology suggests that the band-shaped umbo (a distinctive La Tène II type) was in use by 229 BC (de Navarro 1977: 128, with the correction from Hollstein 1980: 77; before dendrochronological dates were available, de Navarro 1972: 316 suggested that the band-shaped umbo went back to at least c. 225 BC!). Cernon-sur-Coole would seem to date from the middle to late third century.

Much of Style V is contemporary with much of La Tène III. Even if the correlation was exact, it would be difficult to suggest an absolute date: 'the lower limit of Middle and the upper limit of Late La Tène is perhaps the most baffling problem in La Tène chronology' (de Navarro 1972: 317). In a full discussion of the evidence then available, de Navarro (ibid.) was inclined to correlate the start of La Tène III on the Swiss plateau with the appearance of the Nauheim brooch and a date of c. 60 BC. Today there is evidence that the Nauheim brooch extended back in the south of France into the second century BC and was in use for much of the first century BC (Feugère 1981: 310-13). For the present purposes it is difficult to improve on the schematic dates for the duration of La Tène II which de Navarro suggested long ago as a modification of Déchelette's dates: 250± to 120-BC (de Navarro 1936: 19).

So, where in this sequence of Early Celtic Art in Britain does the Battersea shield belong? Most scholars have been impressed with the fold-over symmetry of its design, which they have taken as a hint of Roman influence. Hawkes (1933: 153) detected the influence of Augustan metalwork and referred specifically to the Hildesheim treasure (cf. Pernice & Winter 1901); Jacobsthal (above p. 25) also mentioned Hildesheim; and Fox (1958: 94, pl. 59a and b) turned to the same source as a possible influence on some mirror designs. Certainly that art-style was known on the banks of the Thames, for there is an excellent example on a repoussé plaque on the sheath of the Fulham sword (Fig. 11; Smith 1918: 26, fig. 25: 1922a: 80, fig. 101) an Augustan/Tiberian gladius of Mainz type (Ulbert 1969) found in the river in 1873. But symmetry played an important part in Early Celtic art long before the Augustan period. The repoussé-work on the Wandsworth round boss is symmetrical; the Wandsworth mask boss and Witham shield have designs arranged symmetrically across a diagonal line; dragon-pairs are identical confronted motifs; the Wisbech scabbard and Cerrig-y-Drudion 'bowl' carry symmetric designs; and the simple Style I ornament is always evenly balanced.

The dominant repoussé forms on the Battersea shield are the palmette and interlocking S-motifs. Both occur early in the development of Early Celtic art on the Continent, and the palmette in particular was popular in Early Style art in Champagne. Its use on a flat circular field is seen on the larger disc from Ecury-sur-Coole (Fig. 12a; Jacobsthal 1944: no. 189), which provides an interesting comparison with the palmette on the central part of the

Period	Sheaths	Scabbards medium	Scabbards long	Brooches
Hallstatt D c. 450 BC — La Tène I	Minster Ditch I Wandsworth I Hammersmith I Hammersmith I	Orton Meadows I Wisbech I Standlake II Battersea (dragon pair) Hammersmith (dragon pair) Witham IV		Wood Eaton I Hammersmith I Hunsbury I Box I
c. 250 BC — La Tène II		Bann IV Fovant IV Little Wittenham IV Sutton IV		Newnham Croft III (associated with II) Sawdon IV Danes Graves III Beckley II? Wood Eaton II?
c. 120 BC — La Tène III		Bugthorpe V Grimthorpe V	Henley IV/V Little Wittenham V Hunsbury V Meare V Amerden V Isleham V	
AD 43 — Roman				Birdlip (associated with V) Polden Hill Santon Downham

Table II Sequences of decorated sheaths/scabbards and brooches (each with its numbered art style) roughly related to chronological periods.

Battersea shield (Fig. 12b). Both are enclosed by a curved frame; the central lobe-like leaves are similar – both surmounted by a central point; and the bases are similar in shape though not in filling. The Ecury side-leaves are interlocked with corresponding motifs in a yin-yang device whereas at Battersea the place of the side-leaves has been taken by applied roundels. The palmettes at Ecury are essentially four separate motifs, but when they are linked in a frieze, as on the Canosa helmet (Fig. 12c; Jacobsthal 1944: no. 156, PP. 466-7) which is in the same tradition as the Champagne pieces, they can incorporate the triangular linking motif which occurs four times on the central panel of the Battersea shield (Fig. 12d). The motif described as 'horns' (Fig. 12g) can be matched on the Besançon flagon (Fig. 12f; Frey 1955) – another work closely related to the Champagne pieces – and again the yin-yangs of the Continental piece are replaced by roundels. Spratling (unpublished comments) prefers to see the design on Panel A as a symmetrical arrangement across a diagonal instead of a vertical or horizontal line. Be that as it may, when thus viewed (Fig. 13a) there is an obvious similarity with the design on the Witham boss (Fig. 13b) which also has a palmette leading into a hollow-sided triangle and then a double-circle motif. The Witham design might well

be derived from Early Style floral art via the design on Panel A.

The interlocking S-motif which dominates the two end-panels on the Battersea shield cannot be paralleled so closely. On an elongated field it occurs, of course, on the Wisbech scabbard, where it arises from the side-petals of a palmette (cf. Jacobsthal 1944: pl. 271), but its use in a circular field (other than in triskeles and whirligigs) is more unusual. There is a somewhat similar use of the motif on the bronzes from 'La Bouvandeau', Somme-Tourbe (Jacobsthal 1944: no. 171, P. 343).

The basic design on the Battersea shield could have been created at an early stage but the technique of production, large scale and highly skilled repoussé, is not at all easy to match. Most La Tène metalwork on the Continent is decorated by casting, engraving/chasing or low relief repoussé, but high relief repoussé operations seem to be limited to the British Isles. Jope (1976: 169-70) saw the high relief of the Wandsworth mask boss as a translation from solid cast bronze works on the Continent. For details of the repoussé he pointed to 'bird-askoi' (at least two) from a grave at Castiglione delle Stiviere, near Sirmio on Lake Garda (ibid.: fig. 6d; Jacobsthal 1944: no. 398). In his comments on those Italian pieces Jacobsthal (ibid.: 110) noted an affinity with the other (round) Wandsworth boss, and Fox (1958: 24) drew the same 'bird-askoi' into his discussion of the Torrs chamfrein. Jacobsthal's discussion of the date of the Sirmio pieces is

Figure 11. Panel of bronze repoussé ornament from the scabbard of the Fulham sword. Scale 1:1.

not very satisfactory: with regard to their affinity with the Wandsworth round boss, 'the chronology of related bird-askoi and the presence in the grave of fifth/fourth-century Etruscan bronzes tell against so late a date: I reserve judgement' (ibid.: 110); and elsewhere, 'the bird-askoi are of a style otherwise unknown which I cannot date, but certainly later, probably much later, than the associated Etruscan bronzes' (ibid.: 146). Jope (1976: 178, n. 25) added hopefully that 'the bird-askoi can hardly be isolated work'. Recent research by de Marinis and Tizzoni suggests that these bronzes belong to a carnyx, but they have found nothing comparable in North Italy (information from J.V.S. Megaw). Perhaps the carnyx was an export from Britain!

Another aspect of the Battersea shield which has convinced several scholars that it belongs late in La Tène III is the form and composition of the decorative roundels which have been compared with those from the Lexden Tumulus (Laver 1927: 250, pl. xv, fig. 1) and Hertford Heath (Hüssen 1983) – two burials dating from the decades around the year AD 1. The roundels from those two sites are slightly different from Battersea, in that the frames seem to have been cut from sheet bronze and not cast, and they have been secured only by adhesive or solder and not riveted. These differences are not significant chronologically, however, because a roundel from Hod Hill, with cast frame and rivet hole, has similar red 'enamel' inlay but also discs of blue glass which suggests a date in the first century AD (Brailsford 1962: fig. 14, I. 26; for analyses of the red 'enamel' in the roundels from Battersea, Hertford Heath, Lexden and Hod Hill see Hughes 1972). But that should not be the end of the argument, because half a century ago Henry (1933: 81) pointed out that *'les boutons du bouclier de Battersea sont exactement construits comme les bouchons des oenochoes de Basse-Yutz'*. Analysis has confirmed that the red 'enamel' of the Basse-Yutz lids is very similar to the others (p. 50); the Basse-Yutz frames have been cast but the roundels have not been secured by rivets. This comparison extends the date range for such artefacts very considerably, for the most recent opinion puts the Basse-Yutz flagons in the fifth century BC (J.V.S. Megaw, in a lecture at Oxford, 1983).

Red 'enamel' is known in other early contexts on the Continent (Jacobsthal 1944: 133-4) but in Britain it is mainly late. According to Smith (1918: 22) there were traces of red 'enamel' at one time in the decoration on the Brentford 'horn-cap' of which Fox (1958: 3) detected 'one blob – almost microscopic', but none of it survives today and the very smooth base of the sunken area would have provided no key for enamel. The Brentford palmette-derived design (Fig. 12e) may be compared with that on the central panel of the Battersea shield (Fig. 12d), but the comparison is of little help for chronology because not only is the Brentford 'horn-cap' an unassociated find from the Thames, but it is also of disputed date. It was regarded by de Navarro (1952: 73) as an excellent example of the Waldalgesheim Style, and he maintained this view (1972: 275) in spite of Jope (1961a: 78) who would put it in the

Figure 12. Designs on the Battersea shield (b, d and g) and other pieces: a. Ecury-sur-Coole (after Jacobsthal 1944, no. 189); c. Canosa (after ibid. no. 156); e. Brentford (after Fox 1958, pl. 4); f. Besançon (after Frey 1955: pl. VIII).

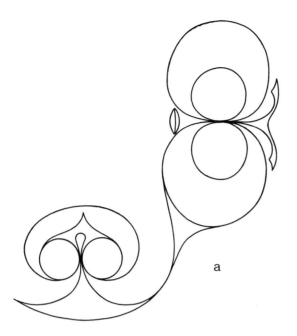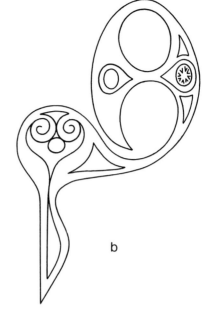

Figure 13. Designs on the Battersea shield (a) and the Witham shield (b).

first century BC or later. Frey & Megaw (1976: 54-5) think that it is derived from the Waldalgesheim Style, and not earlier than the middle of the third century.

There are several minor examples of Styles I and II in Britain, so the appearance of a major work should not be unexpected. Study of the decoration of the Battersea shield suggests that there is a case for considering a relatively early date, but how does that tally with the form of the shield itself? Other writers have held that both the shape of the shield and the appearance of the circular boss are late features, so it is necessary to look now at the history of the Celtic shield.

iii *The Celtic Shield*

Only two La Tène shields are entirely faced with bronze, which not only preserves their exact shapes but also their entire schemes of decoration, and both of them were found in Britain. Together with other significant remains including decorated pieces, they ensure that Britain plays an important role in any discussion of Celtic shields. But the wealth of material is somewhat offset by the circumstances of discovery, for most of the best decorated pieces are unassociated and even where they have been found in hoards the hoards are either of disputed date (Tal-y-llyn) or possibly accumulative (Llyn Cerrig Bach). Of the simpler shield-bosses several have been found in graves, but most seem to be La Tène III in date (Great Brackstead, Grimthorpe, Owslebury, St Lawrence and Snailwell), one is Roman (Stanfordbury) and there are three from a Roman hoard (Polden Hill). No British shield or shield-boss has La Tène I or II (or Hallstatt C or D) associations.

The situation is different on the Continent, where metal remains of shields are found in graves throughout the La Tène period and the overall sequence of development can be established. Champagne is particularly important from this point of view, because for much of the first millennium BC (and indeed later) there is an unbroken sequence of burials often generously equipped with grave-goods. Warriors and their accoutrements are well represented, and the development of shields there seems representative of western Europe. Although the sequence of graves is still inadequately explored, a rudimentary framework exists, and for the current study Champagne has the additional advantage of being not too far distant from Britain.

The best-known La Tène shield-boss is of band-shaped form (Fig. 14: 6-9) and was used throughout Europe. The shield itself would have been made of organic materials – wood and perhaps leather – so it survives only in exceptional circumstances. But waterlogged examples from Scandinavia and Switzerland, one from the dry sands of North Africa, as well as representations and models, give a good idea of the organic form which has perished in the Champagne chalk (Rosenberg 1937: 48-61, 106-9; Vouga 1923: 59-62; Kimmig 1940 – but see Krämer 1950: 355 and Maier 1973: 471 on the date of the Faiyum shield). In Champagne the shape of the shield whose umbo was band-shaped is indicated by sketch-plans published by André Brisson and the surviving remains of metal edgings. There seem to have been two types: one has at least one squared end and outwardly bowed sides (Fère-Champenoise *'le Fin d'Ecury'* t.7, Brisson 1935: 76, fig p. 74; Gourgançon *'St Mard'* t.9, Brisson & Loppin 1938: 24, fig. 3, left); and the other has a rounded end (Fère-Champenoise *'le Fin d'Ecury'* t.8, Brisson 1935: 76, fig. p.

75: Fère-Champenoise 'le Fauborg de Connantre' t.58, Brisson et al. 1970: pl. viii). Judging from the organic remains there would have been a spindle-shaped boss placed vertically to cover a circular or oval hole in the centre of the shield – on the back this hole would have been crossed horizontally by a handle, so that the hand that gripped it would be accommodated under the boss (cf. Pl. XI). The hand-space was protected, and the boss secured, by the band-shaped umbo whose wings were nailed to the body of the shield. This type of boss made its appearance in Europe at the start of La Tène II, and there is reason to suppose that it was used at La Tène itself by 229 BC (de Navarro 1977: 128, with correction from Hollstein 1980: 77). In Champagne it seems to have appeared at the same time as the La Tène II brooch but before the typical La Tène II sword (Stead 1983: 492).

Several different types of band-shaped umbo can be distinguished, varying especially in the shape of the wings (e.g. Rapin 1982: fig. 14) – rounded (Fig. 14: 7), trilobate (Fig. 14: 6), squared (Fig. 14: 8) or flared – and at least one type, whose boss has sharply-raised edges at top and bottom, was used well into La Tène III (Fig. 14: 9). But there are few La Tène III warrior-burials in Champagne, and even when swords are among the grave-goods shield-bosses are not always present. One La Tène III (or Gallo-Roman 'précoce') grave has a circular boss, a type which seems to have replaced the band-shaped umbo in the course of La Tène III. That grave, at Clamanges, was devoid of sword and spear-heads but can be dated by a bronze Kragenfibel (mentioned, Lacroix 1929: 71; illustrated, Stead 1981: pl. 13) – a type which was current in Augustan/Tiberian times (Ettlinger 1973: 71-2).

The shield with circular iron boss appeared elsewhere in Europe about this time or a little earlier. In the Middle Rhineland the earliest circular bosses occur in La Tène D2 contexts (Decker 1968: 51; Polenz 1971: 49-50; Joachim 1974: 163-5) and the band-shaped boss survived to the end of the first century BC. A band-shaped and a round (and conical) boss were found together in an early Augustan cremation at Heimbach-Weiser (Joachim 1973: 33-4, fig. 11, for the date, p. 41). Most round bosses are hemispherical in profile, although some are conical and several terminate in a spike – a type for which a Germanic origin has been postulated (Schönberger 1952: 41). These three types of boss are also found in late pre-Roman Iron Age contexts to the north and east (Hachmann 1960: pl. 14). In Bavaria Krämer (1962: fig. 1) puts the round shield-boss in his D1 phase, and still further to the south-east it occurs in Slovenia in a mixed La Tène C/D horizon (Phase 4 of the Mokronog Group, .e Guštin 1977b: 79; cf. especially grave II at Roji pri Moravčah, Knez 1977: pl. 3). This seems to be the earliest occurrence of an iron round boss in a Celtic grave, but for northern Gaul none can yet be dated before Caesar's wars. The round boss ousted the band-shaped umbo and continued into Roman times, when some were made of bronze and elaborately decorated (Klumbach 1966).

Having followed the development from La Tène II to the time of the Roman Conquest, the history of the La Tène shield must now be traced backwards into La Tène I. At the very beginning of La Tène II there was an alternative to the band-shaped boss in the form of the twinned boss, which consisted of two curved iron plates (Fig. 14: 2) nailed to the sides of the boss. In some areas the twinned boss seems to precede the band-shaped variety (Krämer 1950; de Navarro 1972: 74), but in Champagne there is no independent evidence to give one priority over the other, although the twinned boss was certainly the first to become obsolete (Stead 1983: 492). It seems that the two curved plates were slightly separated, leaving room for the central spine (Roualet et al. 1982: 39, pl. vii), but only in a hybrid variety was the spine itself covered. The hybrid – which combines features of the twinned and band-shaped bosses – is represented by an iron example from Fère-Champenoise 'le Faubourg de Connantre' t.35 (Brisson et al. 1970: pl. iv; a recent study by MM. Roualet and Rapin has yet to be published) and one of bronze from St Etienne-au-Temple (Fig. 14: 4; for its provenance see Stead 1968: 176, n. 5); there are comparable iron fittings on a shield from Horath in the Mosel valley (Kimmig 1938).

Another variation on the twinned boss theme has a spine-cover and two plaques designed to cover the entire length of the spindle-shaped boss. This variety is found in both western (Fig. 14: 3, St Rémy-sur-Bussy, Marne, cf. Klindt-Jensen 1953: 84, fig. 26c; and there is a photograph of another among Baffet Collection archives in the museum at Châlons-sur-Marne) and in eastern Europe (e.g. Holubice in Moravia, Krämer 1950: 357, fig. 3). From a chronological point of view a useful example from the Dürrnberg (grave 39/2, Penninger 1972: pl. 36) is assigned to La Tène A (Pauli 1978: 239, Dürrnberg IIA). It belonged to a rather short 'hide-shaped' shield which has been compared with one represented on a relief from Bormio in the Italian Alps (ibid.: 246; also Pauli 1973). A very similar boss from Letky, near Prague, has been dated to the border-line between La Tène B2 and C (Moucha 1969: 614-15, fig. 4, no. 2) but on the published evidence it would be possible to argue for an earlier date.

The most typical metal fitting from a La Tène I shield in Champagne is the iron handle whose rivet-heads often formed a decorative feature on the front (Fig. 14: 1); indeed many shields are represented by the handle alone (La Cheppe, Stead 1968: fig. 17, nos 1 and 2; St Hilaire-le-Grand and Ecury-sur-Coole, Bretz-Mahler 1959: pl. 100, nos 2 and 4). Curiously, they are only rarely found with band-shaped bosses. La Tène I shields are represented by metal handles in Germany (Haffner 1976: 27) and in Hungary, too, where they have a variety of shaped terminals (Hunyady 1942: pl. xii, 19 and 20; pl. xvi, 12; pl. xlix, 8). But apart from the handles, and pieces of metal edging, there are in Champagne a few fittings of individual types from La Tène I shields. A bronze spine-cover was found in a grave at Etrechy 'le Mont Blanc' along with an iron handle with one surviving bronze-headed rivet and the remains of three or four decorative discs (Morel 1898: 95-9, pl. 19, figs 1-4; Stead 1968: 176-8, fig. 17, nos 2, 4 and 5, with a suggested

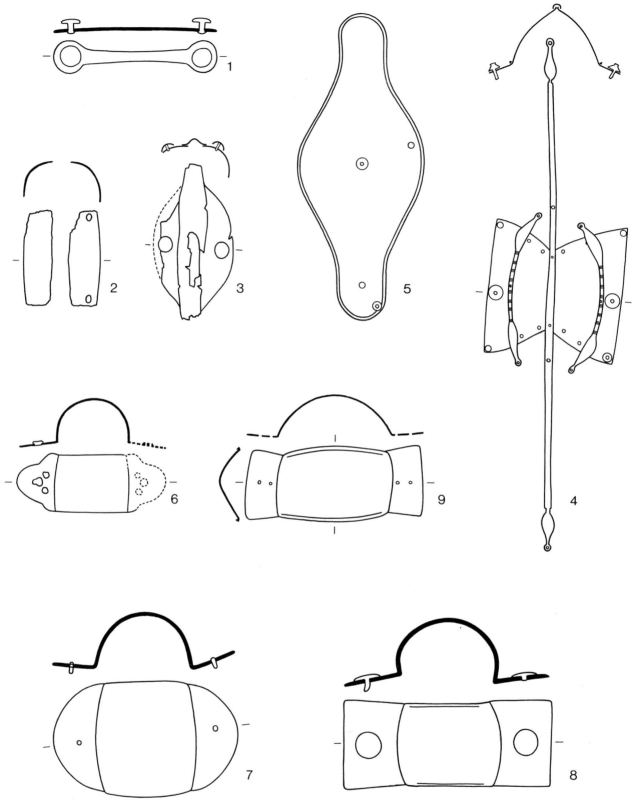

Figure 14. Remains of shields from Champagne: 1, Somme-Bionne (ML 1494); 2, Somme-Suippes (MAN 64466); 3, St Rémy-sur-Bussy (MAN 4884); 4, St Etienne-au-Temple (MAN 18742; after Ritchie); 5, Mairy-sur-Marne (t. 236, after Thierot); 6, Lavannes (MAN 80118E); 7, Connantre (ML 1659); 8, Département Marne (ML 2873); 9, Ville-sur-Retourne (t. VT2). All iron, apart from 4 and the rim of 5 which are bronze. Scale 1:4.

reconstruction, fig. 18b; on the basis of shields found at the Dürrnberg, Pauli 1978: 242, fig. 32, has suggested that the fittings belonged to a much smaller shield). The Etrechy fittings have been compared with some from a short shield of individual shape found with an inhumation at Nový Bydžov in Bohemia (Moucha 1974). The Nový Bydžov fittings comprise two separate lengths of spine-cover separated by a very long strip across the centre of the umbo to form a bronze cross dividing the shield into quadrants each bearing a decorative motif. Moucha suggested a La Tène B date and an origin in Champagne.

There is a rather similar but shorter cruciform arrangement of iron fittings on a shield from a La Tène B cemetery at Ménfőcsanak in Hungary (Uzsoki 1970). It had been decorated with four discs recalling those on the Letky shield and on one from Sulejovice in Bohemia (Moucha 1969: fig. 5, for a reconstruction of both shields). The Bohemian shield-discs (three survived from Letky but there were only two at Sulejovice), richly embellished with coral, have been compared with a pair of similar coral discs from the vicinity of the Camp de Châlons (ibid.: 608-11; Jacobsthal 1944: no. 345) – almost certainly from a burial and on this analogy perhaps from a shield.

Finally, a bronze and iron object from a cart-burial at Mairy-sur-Marne (t.236) has been published as an umbo (Bérard 1913: 115-16, fig. 13; Pauli 1978: 243): certainly weapons were found in the grave – a dagger and three spearheads – and it is difficult to envisage another function for this particular object. Unfortunately it does not survive (or its whereabouts are unknown, in private hands, with other pieces from the Thierot Collection). However, there is a better record than the rough sketch published by Bérard, because it is illustrated full size in an album of coloured drawings preserved at the museum at Châlons-sur-Marne (Fig. 14: 5 is taken from that illustration, by kind permission of M. Ravaux). Depicted in plan only, it evidently consisted of an iron sheet roughly spindle-shaped but with very broad rounded ends, bordered by a narrow edge of bronze shown as about 3 mm wide; measured from the drawing it is 323 mm long. According to Bérard it was 'légèrement bombée' and had 'quelques clous ou rivets sur les bords': the illustration shows the heads of four nails (one central), two of which are labelled in pencil 'gros clou'. Pauli suggested a date at the end of La Tène A or beginning of La Tène B on the basis of the horse-bits but the dagger, a more reliable criterion for chronology, is a Hallstatt D type (Bérard 1913: 113, fig. 8). Bronze fragments from an Early La Tène cremation burial at Kolaje, Bohemia, may have entirely covered a spindle-shaped boss in a rather similar way (Pauli 1978: 243-4).

This review of the remains of Continental shields suggests that the situation in Champagne was fairly typical of the rest of Celtic Europe. The earliest umbo, if indeed it is an umbo, is the unique example from a Late Hallstatt grave at Mairy-sur-Marne. The remains from a La Tène I grave at Etrechy are unmatched in Champagne but resemble fittings in Bohemia, and Bohemian parallels suggest that coral-ornamented discs from one of the cemeteries around the Camp de Châlons also decorated a

shield. Other La Tène I shields in Champagne are known from metal handles and edgings. On analogies from central and eastern Europe a La Tène I date may be suggested for the iron boss from St Rémy-sur-Bussy and another from near Châlons-sur-Marne, and this type is the forerunner of the twinned boss. The band-shaped boss was introduced about the same time as (perhaps slightly later than) the twinned boss at the start of La Tène II, and continued in fashion until it was replaced by the round boss towards the end of the first century BC.

Only a very few of the British remains can be related directly to the Continental sequence. The iron round (and conical) boss from a grave at Snailwell (Fig. 15:1) is closely comparable to the Continental type; the grave included Gallo-Belgic wares and dates from the first half of the first century AD (Lethbridge 1953). Contrary to previous reports the Snailwell boss does have nail-holes in the flange: two survive as perforations and three more can be distinguished on radiographs (Mary Cra'ster very kindly arranged for the radiographs to be taken). But the boss had been stripped from the shield before being placed in the grave – there were no nails in the holes – and as at Clamanges (and indeed Stanfordbury) the shield was not accompanied by weapons.

Two iron hemispherical spiked objects from Hunsbury published as umbos (Dryden 1885: 7, pl. iii, 5; Brown 1915: pl. xxiii, 7; Fell 1936: 26) are oddities, but they are certainly not shield bosses, neither Iron Age nor Anglo-Saxon. An accompanying hemispherical object of the same size (Dryden 1885: 7, pl. iii, 6) has an internal spike, and it looks very much as if one of the 'umbos' has the remains of another internally-spiked hemisphere inside it: they seem to be two pairs designed to fit into one another, but their purpose (? industrial) is obscure. The supposed iron umbo found with brooches of the first half of the first century AD at Sutton Courtenay could have been circular, but it was never illustrated and is now lost (Whimster 1979).

There are fragments of only one iron band-shaped boss, from the remains of a cremation grave at Great Brackstead, Essex, where it was accompanied by a La Tène III sword and scabbard (to be published by C. Going and K. Rodwell). The Great Brackstead umbo has sharply raised edges of the type also found in Continental La Tène III contexts (cf. Fig. 14:9). A band-shaped umbo in bronze, with markedly flaring wings (Fig. 15:2), was found in a grave at Owslebury dated by the excavator early in La Tène III (Collis 1968: 25-7; 1973: 126-9). The boss is surmounted by a spike, which suggests influence from the same feature on some Continental round bosses, and like Great Brackstead it has markedly upturned edges. In some ways the bronze boss from a Claudian burial at Stanfordbury is very similar: it too has upturned edges and its conical top has been surmounted by a button (or spike?), but only a very small part of one wing survives (Dryden 1845: 16, no. 4; Stead 1967: 55, no. 13; Spratling 1972: no. 317).

Several British shields have spindle-shaped umbos covered entirely in metal. In a way they resemble the type represented by St Rémy-sur-Bussy (Fig. 14:3) but the

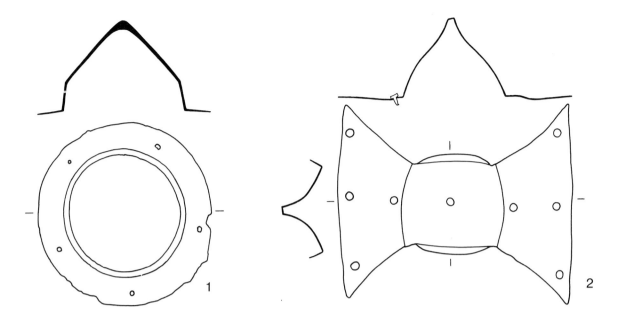

Figure 15. English shield-bosses: 1, Snailwell; 2, Owslebury
(after Spratling). 1, iron; 2, bronze. Scale 1:4.

spine is not defined over the centre of the boss, so the nearest approach on the Continent is represented by the possible examples from Kolaje and Mairy (Fig. 14:5). However, some of the British pieces date very much later than that: an iron umbo from St Lawrence was found with a La Tène III sword (Jones & Stead 1969) and one in bronze from Llyn Cerrig Bach is decorated in Style V (Fox 1946: 7-11, 91). Part of a bronze umbo of this type from South Cadbury Castle has Style IV repoussé decoration: it 'is almost certainly associated with a workshop of the Late Pre-Roman Iron Age, i.e. first century BC or early first century AD, where it was deposited as scrap after being torn off its shield and cut in two' (Spratling 1970b: 22), but the dating evidence has yet to be published in full. The Wandsworth mask shield (Jope 1976), and indeed the Witham shield (Jope 1971), has the spindle-shaped boss completely covered in a similar way.

A closely-linked group of British shield fittings have bronze covers which give more emphasis to the full length of the spine, and it is tempting to link them with the Etrechy shield and its relatives in eastern Europe. The boss from Moel Hirradug (Hemp 1928) is in some way similar to those from St Lawrence and Llyn Cerrig Bach, but the spine-covers are longer; there are resemblances with the Stanfordbury boss, too, particularly in the mouldings above and below the centre. Hemp thought that its peltoid plaque (one survivor of a presumed pair) was derived from the wings of a Continental band-shaped umbo, and doubtless he would have seen the Owslebury boss as an intermediate form. The peltoid plaques relate Moel Hiraddug to the first Tal-y-llyn shield, whose claims to a relatively early date have been championed by Savory (e.g. 1964, 1971, 1976) but disputed by Spratling (1966),

and also to the large curved plaques on the Grimthorpe shield (Stead 1968: 167-9). Whatever the date of the Welsh shields, Grimthorpe is firmly linked by its circular repoussé disc to Style V art, but its long narrow spine-covers would seem to descend from something like the La Tène I shield found at Etrechy. Another shield with long narrow spine-covers was found in the North Grimston grave (Stead 1979:57), and it has been suggested that yet another Yorkshire burial, from Bugthorpe, had a shield represented by decorative discs which might be related to those from the vicinity of the Camp de Châlons (ibid.: 59 – 60).

Apart from one round boss and two, perhaps three, band-shaped bosses which relate well to the Continental sequence, the other pieces discussed so far belong to a distinctive British tradition whose roots lie somewhere among the Continental shields with spindle-shaped umbos. Diagrammatic flow-charts can be constructed (Stead 1968: fig. 18), reversed (Savory 1971: fig. 16; 1976: fig. 1) and rejected (Buckland 1978: 263), but however the matter is viewed the Continental links are weak and the Insular tradition is strong. The Battersea shield is related to this tradition by its terminal panels and the 'animal-heads' supporting the central panel. On the Witham shield there are similar circular panels, each with broad decorated flange and a central hemispherical boss (one damaged and lacking the middle) dished in the centre and with a central decorative roundel. They have been formed from the same sheet of bronze as the central boss. The Witham 'animal-heads' '(equine or bovine to taste), doing duty perhaps like the gorgoneion as ghost-layers' (Jope 1971: 62) face in towards the boss of the shield because they link the broader terminal panels with the narrower spine; the Battersea 'animal-heads' face outwards, because the central panel is larger than the end panels. The Wandsworth mask shield must have had a similar arrangement: it overlapped bronze sheeting, and its surviving end has been lapped by a presumably circular panel (cf. Smith 1905: 93; Jope 1976: fig. 1b). The terminal mask corresponds in position with the Witham 'animal-head', looking inwards, but merges with the much shorter spine. Smith (1905: 93) considered the typology of these shield-bosses and detected a tendency 'for the terminal discs to approach the centre, where the pointed oval expanded into a circular boss with broad flat edging' – the sequence being Witham – Wandsworth mask – Battersea, perhaps with Grimthorpe representing an intermediate stage in the evolution of the round boss. As for the origins of the terminal panels, Smith was content to leave them as 'a native feature' (ibid.), but when discussing the length of the Grimthorpe shield he used the analogy of Battersea to suggest that a disc from the Grimthorpe grave was one of a pair which had been placed at the ends of the spine (ibid.: 104). Hemp (1928: 259 and figs 11 and 12) developed this idea, and whilst admitting that there was 'no absolute authority for placing these studs as they are shown in the drawing' he seemed convinced that there were two discs – a mistake since repeated several times. Thus Hemp derived Battersea from Grimthorpe but saw the Witham shield and Wandsworth mask shield as an independent development. Savory (1976: fig. 1) returned to Smith's sequence, deriving Battersea and Grimthorpe from Witham. But it must be emphasised that there was only one disc in the Grimthorpe grave: it may well have decorated a shield, but on Continental analogies it is more likely to have been in a quadrant than at the end of the spine (Stead 1968: 169, 178; 1979: 59-60). A miniature votive bronze shield from Worth was reconstructed with three bosses along the lines of the Battersea and Witham shields (Smith, in Klein 1928: 79-81, fig. 11, no. 3) but the surviving fragment could be interpreted in other ways. Model shields from Britain seem to be oval or rectangular, with central oval or circular bosses (Stead, in Wacher 1977: 6-7; ibid. 1971: pl. 4d; Leahy 1980). The terminal panels on the Battersea shield are related only to those on the Witham shield (Pl. XIV) and those presumed on the Wandsworth mask shield, but the typological sequence implied by that relationship is obscure.

There are other British shield-bosses, however, to which the Battersea shield is in some way related. The most obvious is the Wandsworth round boss (Pl. XV; Brailsford 1975a: 14-18), a bronze hemispherical boss, dished in the centre, and surrounded by a wide flange. It has repoussé and engraved ornament on the flange, and engraved ornament on the boss. The overall shape very closely resembles that of the central panel on the Battersea shield (Fig. 16) and it seems very likely that this Wandsworth boss also decorated a shield which had other bronze fittings. Smith (1905: 93) suggested that it belonged to a shield like Battersea and Jope has reconstructed it thus (1978: fig. 2a), but if that was so then the bronzes were attached in a quite different way. There is no

hint of the edges of bronze sheets on the underside of the boss, and its rough edge (cf. the ribbed edge of the corresponding panel on the Battersea shield) suggests that it was overlapped and not overlapping. It has four rivet-holes in the middle of the flange – arranged roughly at the corners of a rectangle like Battersea (Fig. 17); a series of sixteen rivet-holes spaced round the edge (at intervals of 54 to 72 mm) but apparently not symmetrical to the orientation of the shield; and two rivet-holes inside the edge, roughly but not exactly at top and bottom (judging the orientation by the four central rivet-holes). The overlap has been defined on the top of the flange by a broad groove, and some of the rivet-holes have clipped the edge (one has missed the edge completely) – showing that they had been knocked through an overlapping layer when the craftsman could not see the edge of the circular panel. The continuous series of roughly equidistant rivets suggests, but does not prove, a continuous border – it is possible that the Wandsworth round boss was no more than a buckler and all that has been lost is a rounded binding, but such a binding could have been attached by far fewer than sixteen rivets.

A second comparable bronze boss is not so well-known, but it too was found in the Thames. Its provenance is given as near the Crab Tree (i.e. Fulham) and it was purchased by the British Museum in 1865. The Fulham boss (Fig. 18) is also circular, hemispherical in profile and with a dished centre – but there the similarity ends because instead of a circular flange with repoussé ornament this boss has a cruciform frame with four broad wings each decorated with a circular disc. Originally published by Franks (1866: 237), who thought 'it may possibly have been part of a breast-plate', it appeared in the first edition of the Iron Age Guide in which Smith too thought that it 'belonged more likely to a breast-plate than to a shield, the two rivets being too short for attachment to wood or stout leather. The ornamental discs in the side limbs are not actual rivet-heads; and the depression in its centre renders the boss unsuitable to protect the shield hand' (Smith 1905: 95). After that it disappeared into obscurity, receiving no more attention until Spratling included it in his comprehensive thesis (1972: no. 306). He classified it as a shield-boss, but could not 'see how the object could have been satisfactorily mounted, for the only means of attachment are the two rivets on the top and bottom bosses which project a mere 2mm at the back' (ibid.: 529). He wondered if it was unfinished, and in the last resort preferred 'to suspend judgement on this shield-mount; indeed, I wonder whether it really does belong to the late pre-Roman Iron Age' (ibid.: 187). Similar doubts must have led to its omission from the second edition of the Iron Age Guide, and its neglect by other writers, but there seems no reason to question its authenticity (p. 50) and the shape of its central boss does seem to relate it to those from Battersea and Wandsworth (Fig. 16).

Finally, there are the three circular bronze bosses in the Polden Hill hoard (Brailsford 1975b: 228). One is rather conical than hemispherical and has repoussé ornament on its broad flange (Fig. 16d), and the other two are identical

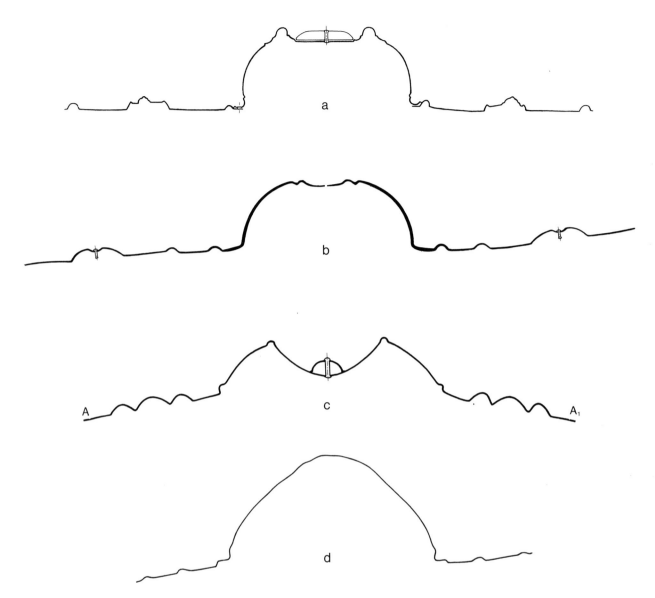

Figure 16.   Profiles of bronze shield-bosses: a. Battersea; b. Wandsworth round boss; c. Fulham; d. Polden Hill. Scale 1:2.

with one another, sharply conical in profile and with equally broad but undecorated flanges. The decorated boss has been attached by four rivets arranged symmetrically at the corners of a square (unlike Battersea and Wandsworth where the distance between rivets is greater in the width than in the height); each of the undecorated bosses has been attached by only three rivets. It has been suggested that the three bosses belonged to a single shield (ibid.: fig. 5, where the outline of the Battersea shield has been used to accommodate them; also Spratling 1972: 185), but there is no reason why they should not belong to three different shields.

Although there is some comparison between the central Battersea panel and the Polden Hill bosses (particularly the one with decorated flange) the profiles are quite different (Fig. 16) and the Polden Hill examples were probably influenced by La Tène III bosses on the Continent. Continental round bosses seem invariably to have been made of iron, but in Britain there are other instances of bronze being used where foreign craftsmen would have preferred iron (e.g. the Owslebury and Stanfordbury bosses). The central part of the Fulham boss is comparable in profile, but its surrounds are very different and it may not have been a shield-boss. Its riveted domes at top and bottom, each within a miniature version of the central dished hemisphere, have a floral design which may be compared with the flower on the similar dome at the centre of the end-panel on the Witham shield (Jope 1971: pls xxiii, xxiva; Brailsford 1975a: pl. 5; cf. also the flowers at the sides of the central boss, Jope 1971: pl. xxii). The domes at the sides are decorated with three touching circles with dotted infilling between, and the

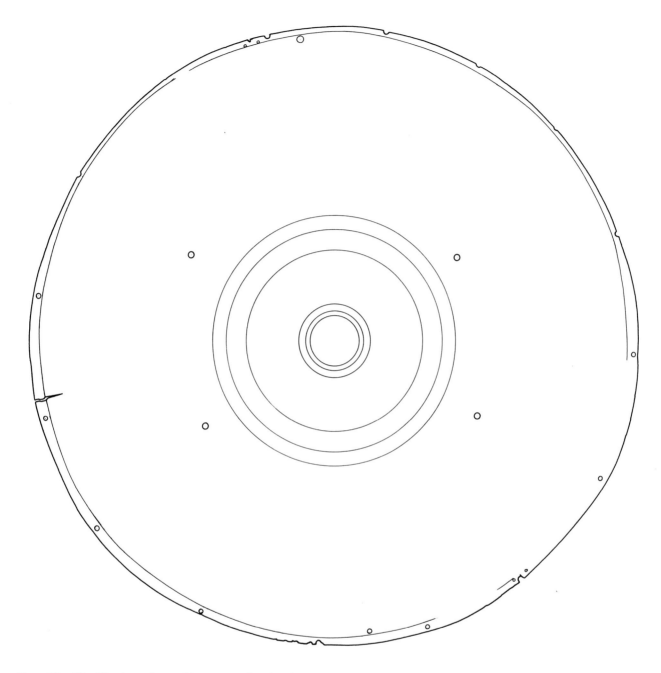

Figure 17. The Wandsworth round boss: an outline drawing to show the rivet-holes. Scale 1:2.

object is edged by a wavy-line bordered by dots – a device used several times in the Early Style art of Champagne (e.g. Jacobsthal 1944: no. 189; Frey 1955: pl. viii) neither of these motifs need be later than Style I. The Fulham boss could belong to La Tène I or II. But the Wandsworth round boss, to which the central panel of the Battersea shield is most closely related, provides much clearer evidence for date. Its engraved ornament stands close to that on the scabbard and shield from the River Witham: it belongs to Style IV and so dates from La Tène II. Hence it is too early to belong to the Continental round boss

tradition, from which it is in any case distinguished by its dished hemispherical boss, broad decorated flange, and construction in bronze instead of iron. The Wandsworth round boss proves an independent development of the circular boss in Britain, represented by only two, perhaps three, examples found unassociated in the River Thames. The origins of this circular boss tradition are obscure, but an ancestry in the native Hallstatt bronze bucklers – perhaps the ritual counterparts of everyday leather shields (Coles 1962: 185) – is not beyond the bounds of possibility. British Iron Age warriors could have used

43

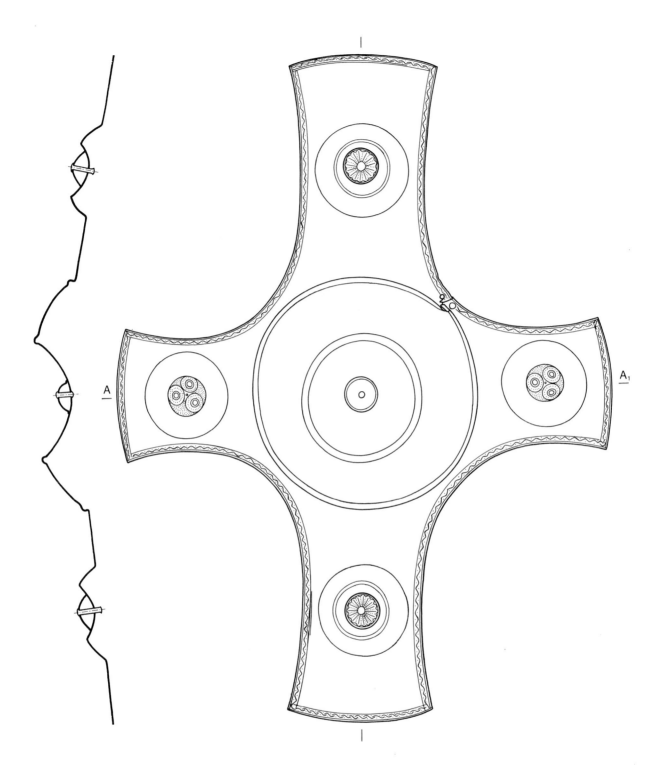

Figure 18.   Bronze boss from Fulham, (for section A – A1 see
Fig. 16c). Scale 1:2.

44

shields of different shapes and sizes made entirely of organic materials, like the one found at Clonoura (Pl. XI; Rynne 1962: pl. xvii, Ritchie 1969: 36-7; Raftery 1983: no. 279), and the surviving metal fittings do not necessarily give a balanced picture. In this respect it is instructive to look at the Certosa situla, which depicts a frieze of warriors carrying three different types of shield (Kastelic 1965: pls 12-15 and 17) – not one of which survives in any other context in the area. In Britain the most relevant representations are of armed cavalry on several British coins dating between the time of Caesar's expeditions and the Claudian conquest. The shield more frequently depicted is long and pointed at top and bottom, sometimes with a circular boss (Pl, XVIa; Allen 1958: 48, pl, I, 9) and sometimes with a spine (ibid. 50, pl. II, 10), but no fewer than four coin-types illustrate circular shields (Pl. XVIb, ibid. 47, pl. III, 21-4). Allen considered that coins of the type shown in Pl. XVIa 'have no Roman features about them and must represent a British warrior'; likewise Pl. XVIb is of a type which does 'not appear to copy any Roman coin model' (ibid.). Small round shields are also carried by warrior-gods depicted on Romano-British altars from King's Stanley, Gloucestershire: three of the gods are obviously intended to represent Mars, but a fourth is rather different because he is not wearing a crested helmet (Pl. XVIc). He has been identified with a god which appears in triplicate (with circular shields) on a votive slab found nearby at Lower Slaughter (O'Neill & Toynbee 1958: 52; cf. also Toynbee 1964: 154, 178; Ross 1967: 184 ff.; Ritchie 1968: 175-6). These carvings in rural Gloucestershire are Romano-British in date but Celtic in character: the shields could be modelled on a local Iron Age type.

Some British shield-bosses from La Tène III and Early Roman graves are related to contemporary pieces on the Continent, but even in La Tène III most British shield-bosses are distinctively Insular and seem to descend from La Tène I traditions on the Continent. Before La Tène III there is very little evidence on which to base the development of the British shield. Two bosses, from Wandsworth, and one complete cover for a shield, from the River Witham, are elaborately decorated in Style IV and so belong to La Tène II: they represent two traditions, the one with a spindle-shaped boss like Continental shields and the other with a circular boss which could be a native form. The Battersea shield can be related to both the Witham shield and the Wandsworth round boss but there is far too little material to give chronological significance to these typological links. There may well have been British shields in La Tène I, but they must have been made entirely of organic materials: in this they would have resembled Continental shields except that they lacked the metal handle which is the sole evidence for a shield in several Continental graves. Nothing is known of the shape of any British La Tène I shield or shield-boss.

Conclusions

Since the Battersea shield entered the British Museum in 1857 it has been subjected to four reconstructions – varying only slightly in the positioning of the binding – on three mounts. The second reconstruction was quite drastic, for new pin-holes were made to secure the bronzes to the mount; new holes may have been created in the first reconstruction, and on both occasions ancient holes were used and could have been distorted. Discounting the modern work, it seems that the principal panels were attached in two slightly different positions in antiquity – which conceivably could have happened in the original assembly. The reconstruction of the shield presents no difficulty, but serious problems have been encountered in the attempt to set it in context.

The development of La Tène shields on the Continent has been examined and where possible British shields have been related to it. This line of enquiry has emphasised the insularity of the British shields, and within the British tradition the Battersea shield is unique. La Tène art provides a more promising approach to chronology – because there are more examples and information can be drawn from different types of artefact. In particular the study of brooches and scabbards has helped to clarify the sequence of British La Tène art – but it is a sequence which does not readily accommodate the Battersea shield. This difficulty may perhaps be explained by the extent of classical influence, which might be attributed to the fussy floral art of Augustan Rome, or the more restrained style derived from Greek-influenced Italy and well represented in Champagne in the fourth century BC.

To counter subjective judgements of art styles and typologies sound objective facts are sorely needed. Several writers have cast the 'enamelled' roundels in this rôle, pointed to parallels especially from the Lexden Tumulus, and seen confirmation for an Augustan date. But the technique of producing the roundels, and the composition of the enamel, can also be matched on the Basse-Yutz flagons which date from the fifth century BC.

The Battersea shield was the work of a highly competent master-craftsman whose hand cannot be recognised in any other extant piece. He certainly worked in Britain, because he used a specifically British form of central circular boss and decorated the three main panels in high relief repoussé, a technique favoured by bronze-workers in Britain but not on the Continent. He employed designs which could have been used in the fourth century BC in a way which reminds some scholars of Augustan art, along with 'enamelled' roundels matched in the fifth and first centuries BC, on an object in some way related to British shields of the third or second centuries BC. Fifty years ago the problem was clearly stated by Leeds (1933: 23): 'There are certain objects – isolated finds, but pieces of obvious importance – which at first sight do not appear to fall easily into line with the most marked tendencies of their time, and thus present difficulties in any attempt to assign them to their proper position in the scheme of Celtic artistic products. The outstanding example that comes to mind is the Battersea Shield'.

Of course, chronology is not the only problem raised by the Battersea shield. Bronze-faced Celtic shields are very rare, for most were more mundane and made entirely of wood or leather. Was this one ever used in war, or was it a parade-piece, or specially made as a trophy or offering? There is nothing to suggest that it was ever used in battle, for the dents and breaks could have occurred in the river or at the time of its recovery, and the slight handle-cover simply tacked to the back would not have survived rough usage. It is conceivable that it was lost in a riverside battle, or that it fell from a capsized boat, but it is just as likely that it was deliberately consigned to the river to placate or honour a Celtic god.

Appendix: Scientific Analyses

The Battersea Shield
Gilding

It is said that gold leaf was found when the shield was dismantled and reassembled in the 1930s (p. 23; Kendrick 1939: 195) but no contemporary report survives. In 1953, after examination in the Research Laboratory 'a spectographic analysis of the gold film and of the bronze beneath it' was reported and it was suggested that the shield had been decorated by mercury gilding. This report was quoted by Brailsford (1956: 760).

When the shield was dismantled in 1969 it was re-examined in the Research Laboratory, and Harold Barker reported: 'A note attached to the 1953 report states that traces of gilding were found on the bronze plates covering the face of the shield, particularly where they had been protected by the U-shaped edging. However, the spectographic examination on which this report was based must have been carried out by an outside institution in 1935-36 when the shield was reconstructed in the Laboratory because there is no record of it in the Laboratory's spectographic files. In view of this, the shield has been examined very carefully for traces of gilding but with completely negative results. Moreover, the trace elements recorded as being present in the bronze in this recent examination (silver, iron and silicon) do not correspond with those previously reported in 1953 (arsenic, antimony, bismuth and mercury). It seems very likely that this discrepancy may be explained by the fact that when the spectographic examination was made by the outside institution there was some confusion with samples from another object which was examined at the same time'.

These findings were confirmed in 1980 when the shield was again examined in the Research Laboratory. Paul Craddock reported: 'A further comprehensive search over all possible areas using energy-dispersive X-ray fluorescence was carried out as part of this work, and once again no trace of gilding could be found. It is therefore most unlikely that the shield was ever gilded'.

The 'enamelled' roundels by Harold Barker (19 March 1969)

The so-called 'enamel' is an opaque red glass, the colour and opacity being due to a suspension of minute crystals of cuprite (cuprous oxide), a red opaque solid, in a clear lead glass. A 3 mg sample of this material was analysed by polarography, and shown to contain 6% of cuprous oxide and 34.2% of lead oxide (see Hughes 1972). This type of glass cannot be melted and fused into place by the normal technique of enamelling: if it is heated to a temperature sufficiently high for it to flow easily, the cuprous oxide in suspension will dissolve in the lead glass, so that the red colour disappears and a green glass is formed. A further difficulty arises from the fact that cuprous oxide is readily oxidised to the black cupric oxide by contact with air at high temperatures. This reaction also causes the red glass to change colour, from red to black, unless it is heated out of contact with the air. These limitations imply that the glass must be heated in a reducing atmosphere to a temperature at which it is soft and pasty but not molten and must then be pressed into place since it is too viscous to flow. With these limitations in mind it is easy to visualise how the roundels on the shield were made. A circular domed fretted piece of metal was made and fitted into a similarly shaped hemispherical depression in a mould of suitable composition (fired clay), the mould was then filled with fragments of the opaque red glass and heated in a reducing atmosphere until the glass just began to soften. The mould was then removed from the furnace and the glass pressed into the fretted piece of metal from the back by means of a suitably shaped tool, perhaps a piece of bronze or even hard charcoal. After cooling, the glass would be backed with pitch or bitumen, a hole drilled through the centre, and the resulting roundel riveted into place on the shield. The red material cannot be regarded as a true enamel, nor as glass cut to shape and inserted using a cloisonné technique.

Quantitative analyses by P.T. Craddock (29 April 1980)

Samples of the sheet metal were taken using a scalpel from the edges of Panels A and B, the handle-cover, the rim and the repaired Sheet D (but not from the repair itself). The samples which weighed between one and five milligrams were analysed by Atomic Absorption Spectrometry using the methods described in Hughes et al. (1976). The precision of the analyses are $\pm < 2\%$ for major elements and $\pm 30\%$ for the trace elements. All quoted elements could be detected to $> 0.01\%$ in the metal.

One of the small cast roundels was also analysed but since this was too small to be destructively sampled, an area was cleaned on the flat back of one of the cells and analysed by energy dispersive X-ray fluorescence. The precision of the analysis is $\pm 5\%$, and elements could be detected to 0.5% in the metal.

The results for the atomic absorption analyses are given in Table III and those for the X-ray fluorescence analysis are:

Copper 85%   Tin 10%   Lead 5%

An approximately 10% tin bronze was used for all the sheet metal components except the rim which contained a little less tin. The trace element contents were also similar with all the components having relatively high iron and arsenic contents: the grip however contains slightly more lead. The overall impression therefore is that all the sheet metal belongs to a common alloy, and that possibly the same stock of metal was used.

The X-ray fluorescence analysis did not record trace elements but showed that the cast roundel was of a leaded tin bronze. There is every likelihood that the lead was deliberately added. Small amounts of lead increase the fluidity of the melt, and this helps the casting of small and intricate shapes. Also, enamel seems to adhere more successfully to leaded copper or bronze, and small amounts of lead were a common additive to Roman and medieval enamelled bronze or copper work.

BATTERSEA SHIELD

	CU	PB	SN	AG	FE	SB	NI	AU	CO	AS	CD	BI	ZN	MN
PANEL A	89.0	.130	10.0	.040	.480	.050	.030		.025	.200		.007	.015	
RIM BINDING	91.0	.060	8.70	.040	.350	.350	.035		.085	.200		.007	.025	
PANEL B	90.0	.050	9.90	.080	.200	.060	.010		.090	.400		.008		
SHEET D	88.0	.050	10.2	.030	.300	.100	.030			.200		.005	.005	.005
HANDLE-COVER	88.0	.310	10.0	.040	.800	.170	.030		.150	.300		.005	.040	

Table III Analysis of samples from the Battersea shield by atomic absorption spectrometry.

Other Objects

Red 'enamel' on the lid of a Basse-Yutz flagon by M.J. Hughes (14 June 1982)

The red 'enamel' in a stud from the lid of one of the flagons was analysed for comparison with the earlier analyses of similar 'enamels' which were carried out in the Research Laboratory. The analysis shows that it is indeed very similar to the previously-analysed examples. The 'enamel' at the back of the stud was analysed using X-ray fluorescence and by comparison with a standard glass, the following approximate composition was arrived at: silica (SiO_2) 35%; potassium oxide (K_2O) 0.2%; calcium oxide (CaO) 2.5%; cuprous oxide (Cu_2O) 13%; lead oxide (PbO) 40%; and tin oxide (SnO_2) 0.1%. (To obtain these figures, it has been assumed that the sum of the sodium, magnesium and other elements in the glass which could not be measured with this apparatus was 10% – i.e. those results given above total 90%.)

When this analysis is compared with those published by Hughes (1972) – in which only lead and copper could be determined – the results look very similar. The average composition was stated to be about 7% cuprous oxide and 25% lead oxide (i.e. a lead/copper ratio of between 3 and 4); the Basse-Yutz 'enamel' has a lead/copper ratio of 3.0 and although the lead and copper are higher than most of the previous results they fall within the range of extremes which were found. It is possible that the difficult nature of the sample – its shape is not ideal for XRF analysis – has led to an underestimation of the silica percentage: the effect of this would be to increase the silica figure above but decrease all the other results (including lead and copper) accordingly. This would not affect the clear fact, however, that the ratio of the copper and lead is typical of those previously-analysed objects.

Examination of the Fulham 'shield-boss' by Susan La Niece (10 March 1982)

The 'shield-boss' is in very good condition. It has a non-crystalline black surface layer (analysed by X-ray diffraction and shown to be mainly dirt) which in places is thin enough to reveal the metal which has a golden patination. It was analysed semi-quantitatively by X-ray fluorescence, with the following results:

Copper 88%   Tin 11%   Lead 1%

This composition is typical of Iron Age metalwork.

Bibliography

ALLEN, D. F., 1958. 'Belgic coins as illustrations of life in the Late Pre-Roman Iron Age of Britain' *Proc. Prehist. Soc.* (24) 43 – 63.

ALLEN, J. Romilly, 1904. *Celtic Art in Pagan and Christian Times.* London.

ATKINSON, R. J. C., & PIGGOTT, S., 1955. 'The Torrs Chamfrein' *Archaeologia* (96) 197 – 235.

BÉRARD, L., 1913. 'Cimetière gaulois de Mairy-Sogny' *Bull. Soc. Arch. Champenoise* 109 – 20.

BOON, G. C., & Savory, H. N., 1975. 'A silver trumpet-brooch with relief decoration, parcel-gilt, from Carmarthen, and a note on the development of the type' *Antiq. J.* (55) 41 – 61.

BRAILSFORD, J. W., 1953. *Later Prehistoric Antiquities of the British Isles* (British Museum). London.

1956. 'Notes on the Battersea Shield and two Iron Age helmets from Britain' *Congress internacionales de ciencias prehistoricas y protohistoricas* (4) Madrid 1954 (1956) 759 – 62.

1962. *Hod Hill* vol. 1. London.

1975a. *Early Celtic masterpieces from Britain in the British Museum.* London.

1975b. 'The Polden Hill hoard, Somerset' *Proc. Prehist. Soc.* (41) 222 – 34.

BRETZ-MAHLER, D., 1959. *La civilisation de La Tène I en Champagne* (*Gallia* supplément, 23).

BRISSON, A., 1935. 'Le Cimetière gaulois de "la Fin d'Ecury" commune de Fère-Champenoise (Marne)' *Bull. Soc. Arch. Champenoise* 72-9.

BRISSON, A., HATT, J.-J., & ROUALET, P., 1970. 'Cimetières gaulois et gallo-romains à enclos en Champagne: 4, Cimetière de Fère-Champenoise, Faubourg de Connantre' *Mems. Soc. d'Agric. … de la Marne* (85) 7 – 26.

BRISSON, A., & LOPPIN, A., 1938. 'Les nécropoles de Gourgançon (Marne)' *Bull. Soc. Arch. Champenoise* 22 – 8.

BROWN, G. BALDWIN, 1915. *The Arts in Early England.* London.

BUCKLAND, P. C., 1978. 'A first-century shield from Doncaster, Yorkshire' *Britannia* (9) 347 – 69.

BULARD, A., 1979. 'Fourreaux ornés d'animaux fantastiques affrontés découverts en France' *Etudes Celtiques* (16) 27 – 52.

CASE, H., & KIRK, J., 1952. 'Archaeological notes 1952' *Oxon.* 17 – 18 (1952 – 3) 216 – 18.

CHARLESWORTH, D., 1973. 'The Aesica hoard' *Arch. Ael.* (5th. ser. i) 225 – 34.

CLARKE, R. R., & HAWKES, C. F. C., 1955. 'An iron anthropoid sword from Shouldham, Norfolk, with related continental and British weapons' *Proc. Prehist. Soc.* (21) 198 – 227.

COLES, J. M., 1962. 'European Bronze Age shields' *Proc. Prehist. Soc.* (28) 156 – 90.

COLLIS, J. R., 1968. 'Excavations at Owslebury, Hants.: an interim report' *Antiq. J.* (48) 18 – 31.

1973. 'Burials with weapons in Iron Age Britain' *Germania* (51) 121 – 33.

CORDER, P., & HAWKES, C. F. C., 1940. 'A panel of Celtic ornament from Elmswell, East Yorkshire' *Antiq. J.* (20) 338 – 57.

COTTON, J., 1979. 'Three Iron Age brooches from the Thames foreshore at Mortlake, Syon and Wandsworth' *Trans. London & Middlesex Arch. Soc.* (30) 180 – 84.

CUMING, H. SYER, 1857. 'On the discovery of Celtic crania in the vicinity of London' *J. Brit. Arch. Ass.* (13) 237 – 39.

1858. 'On further discoveries of Celtic and Roman remains in the Thames off Battersea' *J. Brit. Arch. Ass.* (14) 326 – 30.

DÉCHELETTE, J., 1914. *Manuel d'Archéologie* 2, 3, *Second âge du fer ou époque de La Tène.* Paris.

DECKER, K.-V., 1968. 'Die jüngere Latènezeit im Neuwieder Becken' *Jahrbuch für Geschichte und Kunst des Mittelrheins* (1) 7 – 208.

DE NAVARRO, J. M., 1936. 'A survey of research on an early phase of Celtic culture' *Proc. Brit. Acad.* (22) 297 – 341.

1943. 'A note on the chronology of the La Tène period' in R. E. M. Wheeler, *Maiden Castle, Dorset* (Reports of the Research Committee of the Society of Antiquaries of London, 12) 388 – 94.

1952. 'The Celts in Britain and their art' in M. P. Charlesworth *et al.*, *The Heritage of Early Britain.* London 56 – 82.

1959. 'Zu einigen Schwertscheiden aus La Tène' *Ber. RGK* (40) 79 – 119.

1966. 'Swords and scabbards of the La Tène period with incised laddering' in R. Degen, W. Drack & R. Wyss, eds., *Helvetia Antiqua* (Festschrift Emil Vogt) 147 – 54.

1972. *The finds from the site of La Tène, 1, Scabbards and the swords found in them.* London.

1977. 'Swiss arms of the La Tène period at Princeton, N. J.' in V. Markotic, ed., *Ancient Europe and the Mediterranean.* Warminster 121 – 33.

DENT, J. S., 1982. 'Cemeteries and settlement patterns of the Iron Age on the Yorkshire Wolds' *Proc. Prehist. Soc.* (48) 437 – 57.

DRYDEN, Sir Henry, 1845. 'Roman and Roman-British remains at and near Shefford, Co. Beds.' *Pubs.*

Cambridge Ant. Soc. 1 (1840 – 46) no. 8.
1885. 'Hunsbury or Danes Camp' *Ass. Arch. Soc. Rep.* 18 (1885 – 6) 53 – 61.

DUVAL, P.-M., 1971. 'Les styles de l'art celtique occidental: terminologie et chronologie' *Actes du VIIe Congrès international des sciences préhistoriques et protohistoriques*, Prague 1966, 2 (1971) 812 – 17.
1977. *Les Celtes.* Paris.

DUVAL, P.-M, & HAWKES, C. F. C., 1976. *Celtic art in Ancient Europe: five protohistoric centuries.* London.

ETTLINGER, E., 1973. *Die römischen Fibeln in der Schweiz.* Bern.

EVANS, A. J., 1915. 'Late-Celtic dagger, fibula, and jet cameo' *Archaeologia* 66 (1914 – 15) 569 – 71.

FELL, C. I., 1936. 'The Hunsbury hill-fort, Northants.: a new survey of the material' *Arch. J.* (93) 57 – 100.

FEUGÈRE, M., 1981. *Les fibules de la Gaule meridionale* (doctoral thesis, University of Provence, Aix-en-Provence).

FOX, C., 1927. 'A La Tène I brooch from Wales: with notes on the typology and distribution of these brooches in Britain' *Arch. Camb.* (82) 67 – 112.
1946. *A find of the Early Iron Age from Llyn Cerrig Bach, Anglesey.* Cardiff.
1951. 'The study of Early Celtic metalwork in Britain' *Advancement of Science* 8 (1951 – 2) 184 – 93.
1958. *Pattern and Purpose: a survey of Early Celtic Art in Britain.* Cardiff.

FRANKS, A. W., 1866. 'Additions made to the collection of British antiquities in the British Museum during the year 1865' *Proc. Soc. Ant. London* 2nd ser., 3 (1864 – 7) 233 – 42.

FREY, O.-H., 1955. *Eine etruskische Bronzeschnabelkanne* (Annales littéraires de l'université de Besançon, 2e ser., 2, 1).
1974. 'Akanthusornamentik in der keltischen Kunst' *Hamburger Beiträge zur Arch.* (4) 141 – 57.
1976. 'Du Premier style au Style de Waldalgesheim' in Duval & Hawkes (1976) 141 – 59.

FREY, O.-H., & MEGAW, J. V. S., 1976 'Palmette and circle: Early Celtic Art in Britain and its continental background' *Proc. Prehist. Soc.* (42) 47 – 65.

GUŠTIN, M., 1977a. *Keltske Študije* (Posavski Muzej Brežice, knjiga 4).
1977b. 'Relativna kronologija grobov "Mokronoške skupine"' in Guštin (1977a) 67 – 103.

HACHMANN, R., 1960. Die Chronologie der jüngeren vorrömischen Eisenzeit. Studien zum Stand der Forschung im nördlichen Mitteleuropa und in Skandinavien' *Ber. RGK* (41) 1 – 276.

HAFFNER, A., 1976. *Die westliche Hunsrück-Eifel-Kultur* (Römisch-Germanische Forschungen, 36).

HARDING, D. W., 1972. *The Iron Age in the Upper Thames Basin.* Oxford.
1974. *The Iron Age in Lowland Britain.* London and Boston.

HAWKES, C. F. C., 1933. Review of Leeds (1933) and Henry (1933), *Arch. J.* (90) 150 – 55
1976a. 'Celts and cultures: wealth, power, art' in Duval

& Hawkes (1976) 1 – 21.
1976b. 'Waldalgesheim problems' in Duval & Hawkes (1976) 164 – 5.

HAWKES, C. F. C., and Jacobsthal, P., 1945. 'A Celtic bird-brooch from Red Hill, near Long Eaton, Notts.' *Antiq. J.* (25) 117 – 24.

HEMP, W. J., 1928. 'A La Tène shield from Moel Hirradug, Flintshire' *Arch. Camb.* (7th ser., 8) 253 – 84.

HENRY, F., 1933. 'Emailleurs d'occident' *Préhistoire* (2) 65 – 146.

HODSON, F. R., 1964. 'La Tène chronology, continental and British' *Bull. Institute Arch.* London (4) 123 – 41.
1968. *The La Tène cemetery at Münsingen-Rain* (Acta Bernensia, 5).

HOLLSTEIN, E., 1980. *Mitteleuropäische Eichenchronologie* (Rheinisches Landesmusuem Trier, Trierer Grabungen und Forschungen, 11).

HOLMES, T. RICE, 1907. *Ancient Britain and the invasions of Julius Caesar.* Oxford.

HUGHES, M. J., 1972. 'A technical study of opaque red glass of the Iron Age in Britain' *Proc. Prehist. Soc.* (38) 98 – 107.

HUGHES, M. J., COWELL, M. R., & CRADDOCK, P. T., 1976. 'Atomic absorption techniques in archaeology' *Archaeometry* (18) 19 – 38.

HUNYADY, I., 1942. *Kelták a Kárpát-medencében* (Diss. Pann. 2, 18).

HÜSSEN, C.-M., 1983. *A rich Late La Tène burial at Hertford Heath, Hertfordshire* (British Mus. Occasional Paper, 44).

JACOBSTHAL, P., 1935. 'Early Celtic Art' *The Burlington Magazine* 67 (no. 390, Sept. 1935) 113 – 27.
1939. 'The Witham sword' *The Burlington Magazine* 75 (no. 436, July 1939) 28 – 31.
1944. *Early Celtic Art.* Oxford.

JOACHIM, H.-E., 1973. 'Ein reich ausgestattetes Wagengrab der Spätlatènezeit aus Neuwied, Stadtteil Heimbach-Weis' *Bonner Jahrbucher* (173) 1 – 44.
1974. 'Ein spätlatènezeitliches Reitergrab aus Kollig, Kreis Mayen-Koblenz' *Hamburger Beiträge zur Arch.* (4) 159 – 70.

JONES, J. D., & STEAD, I. M., 1969. 'An Early Iron Age warrior-burial found at St Lawrence, Isle of Wight' *Proc. Prehist. Soc.* (35) 351 – 4.

JOPE, E. M., 1954. 'An Iron Age decorated sword-scabbard from the River Bann at Toome' *Ulster Journ. Arch.* (17) 81 – 91.
1961a. 'The beginnings of La Tène ornamental style in the British Isles' in S. S. Frere, ed., *Problems of the Iron Age in Southern Britain* 69 – 83.
1961b. 'Daggers of the Early Iron Age in Britain' *Proc. Prehist. Soc.* (27) 307 – 43.
1971. 'The Witham Shield' in G. de G. Sieveking, ed., *Prehistoric and Roman Studies* (= Brit. Mus. Quarterly, 35) 61 – 9.
1976. 'The Wandsworth Mask Shield and its European stylistic sources of inspiration' in Duval & Hawkes (1976) 167 – 84.
1978. 'The southward face of Celtic Britain; 300 BC –

AD 50: four British parade shields' *Academia Nazionale dei Lincei* (375) 27 – 36.

KASTELIC, J., 1965. *Situla Art.* London.

KEMBLE, J. M., 1863. *Horae Ferales.* London.

KENDRICK, T. D., 1938. *Anglo-Saxon Art to AD 900.* London.

1939. 'Celtic sword from the River Witham' *Antiq. J.* (19) 194 – 5.

KENDRICK, T. D., & HAWKES, C. F. C., 1932. *Archaeology in England and Wales 1914 – 31.* London.

KIMMIG, W., 1938. 'Ein Kriegergrab der Hunsrück-Eifel-Kultur von Horath, Kr. Bernkastel' in E. Sprockhoff, *Marburger Studien* 125 – 32.

1940. 'Ein Keltenschild aus Agypten' *Germania* (24) 106 – 11.

KLEIN, W. G., 1928. 'Roman temple at Worth, Kent' *Antiq. J.* (8) 76 – 86.

KLINDT-JENSEN, O., 1953. *The Bronze Cauldron from Brå* (Jysk Arkaeologisk Selskabs Skrifter, 3).

KLUMBACH, H., 1966. 'Drei römische Schildbuckel aus Mainz' *Jahrb. RGZM* (13) 165 – 89.

KNEZ, T., 1977. 'Keltski grobovi iz Roj pri Moravčah' in Guštin (1977a) 105 – 25.

KRÄMER, W., 1950. 'Zur Zeitstellung der holzeren Schilde des Hirschsprungfundes' *Prähist. Zeitschr.* 34 – 5 (1949 – 50) 354 – 60.

1962. 'Manching II: zu den Ausgrabungen in den Jahren 1957 bis 1961' *Germania* (40) 293 – 317.

KRUTA, V., 1974. 'Remarques sur l'apparition du rinceau dans l'art celtique' *Etudes Celtiques* (14) 21 – 30.

1977. 'Les fibules laténiennes à décor d'inspiration végétale au IVe siècle avant notre ère' *Etudes Celtiques* 15, 1 (1976 – 7) 19 – 46.

1978. 'Le casque d'Amfreville-sous-les-Monts (Eure) et quelques problèmes de l'art celtique du IVe siècle avant notre ère' *Etudes Celtiques* (15, 2) 405 – 24.

1979. 'Duchcov-Münsingen: nature et diffusion d'une phase laténienne' in P.-M. Duval & V. Kruta (eds) *Les mouvements celtiques du Ve au Ier siècle avant notre ère.* Paris.

1982. 'Aspects unitaires et faciès dans l'art celtique du IVe siècle avant notre ère: l'hypothèse d'un foyer Celto-Italique' in P.-M. Duval & V. Kruta (eds.) *L'art celtique de la periode d'expansion, IVe et IIIe siècles avant notre ère.* (Ecole pratique des hautes études, 3, Hautes études du monde gréco-romain, 13).

LACROIX, L., 1929. 'Procès-verbal de la séance du 9 juin 1929' *Bull. Soc. Arch. Champenoise* 69 – 72.

LAVER, P. G., 1927. 'The excavation of a tumulus at Lexden, Colchester' *Archaeologia* (76) 241 – 54.

LEAHY, K., 1980. 'Votive models from Kirmington, South Humberside' *Britannia* (11) 326 – 30.

LEEDS, E. T., 1933. *Celtic Ornament.* Oxford.

LENERZ-DE WILDE, M., 1977. *Zirkelornamentik in der Kunst der Latènezeit* (Münchner Beiträge zur Vor- und Frühgeschichte, 25).

LETHBRIDGE, T. C., 1953. 'Burial of an Iron Age warrior at Snailwell' *Proc. Cambridge Ant. Soc.* (47) 25 – 37.

MACKRETH, D. F., 1981. 'The brooches' in C. Partridge,

Skeleton Green (Britannia Monograph series, 2) 130 – 51.

MAIER, F., 1973. 'Keltische Altertümer in Griechenland' *Germania* (51) 459 – 77.

MEGAW, J. V. S., 1970. *Art of the European Iron Age.* Bath.

1973. 'The decorated sword-scabbards of iron from Cernon-sur-Coole (Marne) and Drna, Rimacska Sobota (Slovakia)' *Hamburger Beiträge zur Arch.* (3, 2) 119 – 37.

1983. 'From Transdanubia to Torrs: further notes on a gabion of the late Jonathan Oldbuck' in A. O'Conner & D. V. Clarke, *From the Stone Age to the 'Forty-five'.* Edinburgh 127 – 48.

MOREL, L., 1898. *La Champagne souterraine.* Reims.

MOUCHA, V., 1969. 'Latènezeitliche Gräber aus Sulejovice in Nordwestböhmen' *Arch. Rozhledy* (21) 596 – 617.

1974. 'Přispěvek k posnání štítu z doby laténské v Cechach' *Arch. Rozhledy* (26) 445 – 53, 549 – 51.

O'NEILL, H. E., & Toynbee, J. M. C., 1958. 'Sculptures from a Romano-British well in Gloucestershire' *J. Rom. Stud.* (48) 49 – 55.

PAULI, L., 1973. 'Ein latènezeitliches Steinrelief aus Bormio am Stilfser Joch' *Germania* (51) 85 – 120.

1978. *Der Dürrnberg bei Hallein* III (Münchner Beiträge zur Vor- und Frühgeschichte 18).

PENNINGER, E., 1972. *Der Dürrnberg bei Hallein* I (Münchner Beiträge zur Vor- und Frühgeschichte, 16).

PERNICE, E., & Winter, F., 1901. *Der Hildesheimer Silberfund.* Berlin.

PIGGOTT, S., 1950. 'Swords and scabbards of the British Early Iron Age'. *Proc. Prehist. Soc.* (16) 1 – 28.

1970. *Early Celtic Art.* Edinburgh.

PIGGOTT, S., & DANIEL, G. E., 1951. *A picture book of Ancient British Art.* Cambridge.

POLENZ, H., 1971. *Mittel- und spätlatènezeitliche Brandgräber aus Dietzenbach, Landkreis Offenbach am Main* (Stadt und Kreis Offenbach a.M., Studien und Forschungen, N.F., 4).

POWELL, T. G. E., 1966. *Prehistoric Art.* London.

RAFTERY, B., 1983. *A catalogue of Irish Iron Age antiquities.* Marburg.

RAPIN, A., 1982. 'Das keltische Heiligtum von Gournay-sur-Aronde' *Antike Welt* (13, 2) 39 – 60.

RITCHIE, J. N. G., 1968. *Celtic defensive weaponry in Britain and its continental background* (unpublished Ph.D. thesis, Edinburgh University).

1969. 'Shields in North Britain in the Iron Age' *Scottish Arch. Forum* 31 – 40.

ROSENBERG, G., 1937. *Hjortspringfundet* (Nordiske Fortidsminder, 3, 1).

ROSS, A., 1967. *Pagan Celtic Britain.* London & New York.

ROUALET, P., RAPIN, A., FLUZIN, P., & URAN, L., 1982. 'Sépultures du Crayon, à Ecury-le-Repos (Marne)' *Mems. Soc. d'Agric. … de la Marne* (97) 25 – 44.

RUTLAND, R. A., 1972. 'An Iron Age sword and scabbard from the Thames at Henley, Oxon.' *Antiq. J.* (52) 345 – 6.

RYNNE, E., 1962. 'National Museum of Ireland,

Archaeological acquisitions in the year 1960' *Royal Soc. Antiq. Ireland* (96) 139 – 73.

SAVORY, H. N., 1939. 'Early Iron Age' in *V.C.H. Oxon.* (1) 251 – 61.

1964. 'The Tal-y-llyn hoard' *Antiquity* (38) 18 – 31.

1971. *Excavations at Dinorben, 1965 – 9.* Cardiff.

1976. 'The La Tène shield in Wales' in Duval & Hawkes (1976) 185 – 97.

SCHWAPPACH, F., 1969. 'Stempelverzierte Keramik von Armorica' *Fundberichte aus Hessen* (1) 213 – 87.

1973. 'Frühkeltisches Ornament zwischen Marne, Rhein und Moldau' *Bonner Jahrbücher* (173) 53 – 111.

SCHÖNBERGER, H., 1952. 'Die Spätlatènezeit in der Wetterau' *Saalburg Jahrbuch* (11) 21 – 130.

SHERRATT, A., 1983. 'A newly discovered La Tène sword and scabbard' *Oxford J. Arch.* (2) 115 – 18.

SMITH, R. A., 1905. *A Guide to the antiquities of the Early Iron Age* (British Museum). London.

1909a. 'On a Late-Celtic mirror found at Desborough, Northants., and other mirrors of the period' *Archaeologia* (61) 329 – 46.

1909b. 'A hoard of metal found at Santon Downham, Suffolk' *Proc. Cambridge Ant. Soc.* (13) 146 – 63.

1918. 'Specimens from the Layton Collection in Brentford Public Library' *Archaeologia* 69 (1917 – 18) 1 – 30.

1922a. *Guide to Roman Britain* (British Museum). London.

1922b. 'On some recent exhibits' *Antiq. J.* (2) 92 – 104.

1925. *A Guide to the antiquities of the Early Iron Age* (British Museum). 2nd ed. London.

SPRATLING, M. G., 1966. 'The date of the Tal-y-llyn hoard' *Antiquity* (40) 229 – 30.

1970a. 'The Late Pre-Roman Iron Age bronze mirror from Old Warden' *Beds. Arch. J.* (5) 9 – 16.

1970b. 'Bronze shield-mount' in L. Alcock, 'Excavations at South Cadbury Castle, 1969: a summary report' *Antiq. J.* (50) 21 – 2.

1972. *Southern British decorated bronzes of the Late Pre-Roman Iron Age.* (unpublished Ph.D. thesis, London University).

STANFORD, S. C., 1974. *Croft Ambrey.* Hereford.

STEAD, I. M., 1967. 'A La Tène III burial at Welwyn Garden City' *Archaeologia* (101) 1 – 62.

1968. 'An Iron Age hill-fort at Grimthorpe, Yorkshire, England' *Proc. Prehist. Soc.* (34) 148 – 90.

1976. 'The earliest burials of the Aylesford Culture' in G. de G. Sieveking *et al.*, eds. *Problems in Economic and Social Archaeology* 401 – 16.

1979. *The Arras Culture.* York.

1981. *The Gauls: Celtic antiquities from France.* London.

1983. 'La Tène swords and scabbards in Champagne' *Germania* (61) 487 – 510.

1984. 'Some notes on imported metalwork in Iron Age Britain' in S. Macready & F. H. Thompson, eds., *Cross-Channel trade between Gaul and Britain in the Pre-Roman Iron Age* (Society of Antiquaries of London, Occasional Paper, new series, 4).

STEAD, I. M., HARTWELL, A. P., Lang, J. R. S., La Niece, S. C., and Meeks, N. D., 1981. 'An Iron Age sword and scabbard from Isleham' *Proc. Cambridge Ant. Soc.* (71) 61- 74.

SZABÓ, M., 1977. 'The origins of the Hungarian sword style' *Antiquity* (51) 211 – 20.

TOYNBEE, J. M. C., 1964. *Art in Britain under the Romans.* Oxford.

ULBERT, G., 1969. 'Gladii aus Pompeji. Vorarbeiten zu einem Corpus römischer Gladii' *Germania* (47) 97 – 128.

UZSOKI, A., 1970. 'A Ménfőcsanaki kelti pajzs rekonstrukciós kisérlete' *Arch. Ertesitő* (97) 97 – 108.

VOUGA, P., 1923. *La Tène.* Leipzig.

VULLIAMY, C. E., 1930. *The Archaeology of Middlesex and London.* London.

WACHER, J. S., 1977. 'Excavations at Breedon-on-the-Hill' *Trans. Leicestershire Arch. & Hist. Soc.* 52 (1976 – 7) 1 – 35.

WARDMAN, A., 1972. *The Early La Tène brooches of the British Isles.* (unpublished B A thesis, The Queen's University, Belfast).

WHIMSTER, R., 1979. 'A possible La Tène III inhumation from Sutton Courtenay, Oxfordshire' *Oxon.* (44) 93 – 6.

WILLSON, E. J., 1852. (untitled exhibit note) *Proc. Soc. Ant. London* 2 (1849 – 53) 199.

The Plates

PLATE I   Battersea shield: reverse of Panel A

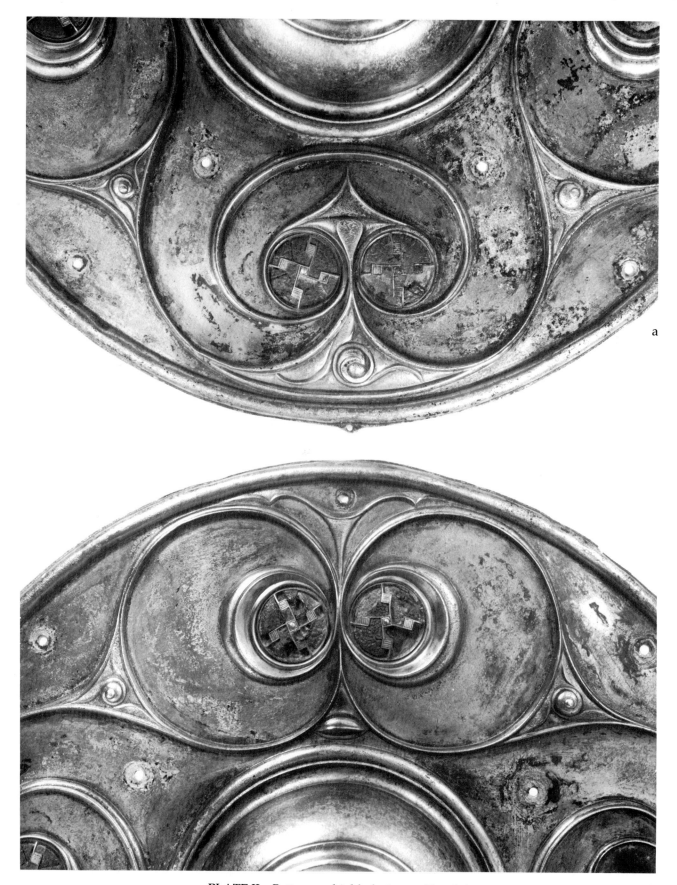

a

b

PLATE II   Battersea shield: design on Panel A

a

PLATE III   Battersea shield: Panel A, details

b

a

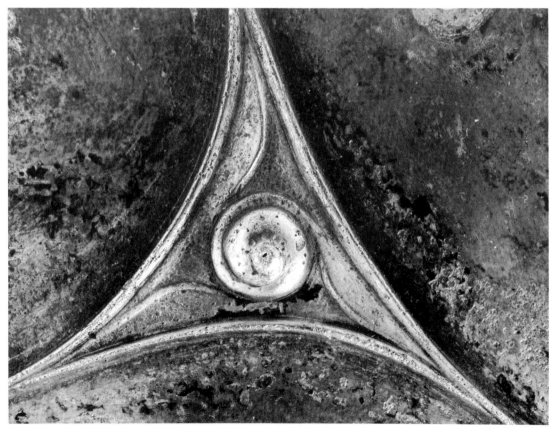

PLATE IV   Battersea shield: Panel A, details

b

a

b

PLATE V Battersea shield: a) Panel A, detail; b) Panel B, detail

PLATE VI   Battersea shield: Panel B

PLATE VII   Battersea shield: reverse of Panel B

a

PLATE VIII   Battersea shield: Panel C, details

b

a

b

PLATE IX   Battersea shield: a) Panel B, detail; b) Panel C, detail

a

b

c

PLATE X   Battersea shield: a) Roundel 10; b) the Henry Roundel; c) reverse of the Henry Roundel

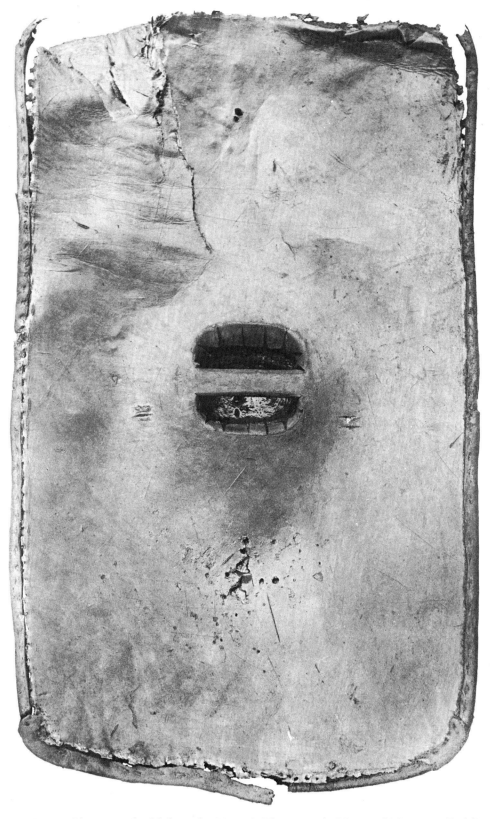

PLATE XI   Clonoura shield (length 570mm). Photograph: National Museum, Dublin

PLATE XII   Battersea shield:
Reconstruction V. Photograph
taken for P. Jacobsthal

PLATE XIII Battersea shield:
Reconstruction Y

PLATE XIV   Witham shield
(length 1130mm)

PLATE XV   Wandsworth round boss (diameter 330mm)

a

b

PLATE XVI

a) Silver coin of Tasciovanus, reverse. Mack 166. Scale ×4

b) Bronze coin of Cunobelinus, reverse. Mack 251. Scale ×4

c) Stone altar from King's Stanley, Gloucestershire (height 605mm)

c